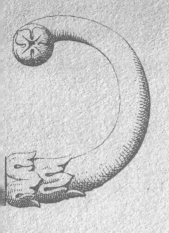

NOSTRADAMUS

THE TOP
100
PROPHECIES

THE ILLUSTRATED
EDITION

NOSTRADAMUS

THE TOP
100
PROPHECIES

THE ILLUSTRATED
EDITION

MARIO READING

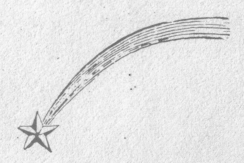

Illustrated by Nicky Ackland-Snow

WATKINS PUBLISHING
LONDON

Nostradamus: The Top 100 Prophecies
The Illustrated Edition
Mario Reading

Distributed in the USA and Canada by
Sterling Publishing Co., Inc.
387 Park Avenue South
New York, NY 10016-8810

This edition first published in the UK and USA in 2010 by
Watkins Publishing
Sixth Floor, Castle House
75–76 Wells Street
London W1T 3QH

Managing Editor: *Christopher Westhorp*
Editor: *Shelagh Boyd*
Designers: *Paul Reid* and *Rebecca Johns* at cobalt id
Picture Research: *Julia Ruxton*
Commissioned artwork: *Nicky Ackland-Snow*

Library of Congress Cataloging-in-Publication Data

Reading, Mario.
Nostradamus : the top 100 prophecies : the illustrated edition / Mario Reading.
  p. cm.
 Includes bibliographical references (p.   ) and index.
 ISBN 978-1-907486-03-6
1. Nostradamus, 1503-1566--Prophecies. 2. Prophecies (Occultism) I.
Nostradamus, 1503-1566. Prophéties. English & French. Selections. II. Title.
BF1815.N8R43 2010
133.3092--dc22

                        2010020391

ISBN: 978-1-907486-03-6

10 9 8 7 6 5 4 3 2 1

Typeset in Granjon Roman
Color reproduction by Scanhouse, Malaysia
Printed in China by Imago

For information about custom editions, special sales, premium and corporate
purchases, please contact Sterling Special Sales Department at 800-805-5489 or
specialsales@sterlingpub.com.

CONTENTS

REVOLUTION, RIOTS and RAPINE 82

ENSLAVEMENT, EXPANSION and EMPIRE 102

FOREWORD

Following the success of my last year's near 1,000-page *The Complete Prophecies of Nostradamus* (Watkins 2009), I was delighted to be asked to prepare the text for a considerably shorter – and in consequence vastly more approachable – illustrated Nostradamus. As part of the preparation process, I was required to choose Nostradamus's 100 best prophecies from his list of 942 published prophecies. This proved easier said than done.

In my first run-through, I came up with a shortlist of 133 absolutely first-rate quatrains – meaning quatrains (i.e. four-line verses) that worked on every possible level – with a back-up list of a further 60 that were, in reality, just as good as the initial 133. I then had to whittle the final list of 193 down to a more manageable 100. In the event, I have managed to sprinkle quite a few bonus quatrains, "tragical, comical, historical, pastoral, pastoral-comical, historical-pastoral, tragical-historical, tragical-comical-historical-pastoral, scene individable, or poem unlimited" *(pace* Polonius) throughout the text, ensuring, I hope, in the process, that readers of this edition will be able to share in my awe at Nostradamus's quite extraordinary historical prescience.

Time and again during these quatrains, the seer makes imaginative leaps that go well beyond the bounds of logic or historical happenstance. The sheer number of his quatrains alone seems cause for wonder, their accuracy simply compounding the surprise one feels on reading, for instance, in his quatrain 9/49 (index number 49, from the 9th of his sequence of 10 *Centuries*), that "the London Parliament will put their king to death". Charles I, of course, was indeed put to death on 30 January 1649, exactly as Nostradamus's index date foretells. And the quatrain? Well that was published in 1568, two years after Nostradamus's own death, and a full 81 years before the event it describes – the equivalent, for instance, of someone living in 2010 making an accurate prediction about events due to occur in 2091. Quite a stretch, you'll agree.

Maybe, you ask, London Parliaments (any Parliaments!) were in the habit, around Nostradamus's time, of putting their kings to death? And therefore, in consequence, the quatrain hardly represents rocket science? Not so. The situation was unprecedented. It simply didn't happen. The only possible explanation for such an uncannily accurate prediction, therefore, can be that Nostradamus had somehow managed to achieve – through God's gift, alchemy, enlightened prescience, spontaneous prognostication, what have you – some degree of cognisance of the future, and was fortunately able to relay it to us, thanks to the invention of the printing press, via the twists and spirals of reported time.

Your next question might be: "Then surely the King Charles quatrain must be a simple one-off? A lucky strike, let's say? Try enough stabs at a prediction, and you're bound to get something right, aren't you?"

Once again, not so. Nostradamus was so completely sure of his subject that he wrote a whole sequence of quatrains about the events surrounding King Charles I's life and predicted death, the English Civil War, and also the life and death of Charles's nemesis, Oliver Cromwell. And, what's more, he linked them all by index date. They include 1/44 – The First English Civil War (1644), 3/44 – Matthew Hopkins Witch-finder General (1644), 8/44 – Queen Henrietta Maria Flees England (1644), 4/45 – Prince Rupert Surrenders Bristol (1645), 2/48 – Oliver Cromwell & The Thirty Tyrants (1648), 9/49 – The Execution of King Charles I (1649), 3/50 – The Stuart Restoration – False Start (1650), and 1/53 – Oliver Cromwell Becomes Lord Protector of England (1653).

And they include this one (please note the analogous index date), which surely vies with 9/49 ("the London Parliament will put their king to death") for sheer, jaw-dropping brilliance:

King Charles I of England

DATE 1649, CENTURY IV, QUATRAIN 49

"Devant le peuple sang sera respandu
Que du haut ciel ne viendra esloigner:
Mais d'un long temps ne sera entendu
L'esprit d'un seul le viendra tesmoigner."

In front of the people blood will be spilled
It will not be far removed from the heavens
But for a long time no one will hear
The spirit of even one person bearing witness.

This is a truly extraordinary quatrain, and with an exact index date, which previous Nostradamian commentators have – somewhat inevitably – ignored. The index date is 49, and refers, of course, to 1649, the year in which King Charles I of England was beheaded on the orders of the 135 commissioners of the House of Commons (republicans and Parliamentarians to a man), of whom 59 signed the actual death warrant. We know that it is a king we are dealing with here for Nostradamus speaks of the "spilled blood" as being "not far removed from the heavens". Charles I, of course, was a staunch (no pun intended) believer in the divine right of kings, which stipulates that a monarch owes his rule directly to the will of God, and that such monarchs are ordained – rather than merely raised – to the throne. Divine right also carried with it the concept of the mandate of "heaven" (to which Nostradamus may be referring), and which harkens back to ancient China, and to the idea that heaven would respond in kind to a just and responsible ruler. The last two lines are pretty much self-evident, as they describe the situation of collective silence (and collective guilt?) in Cromwell's England in the immediate aftermath of the execution, and which continued for a further nine years until the Lord Protector's death. Hearsay has it that a communal moan went up as the anonymous headsman's axe cleaved through the royal vertebrae, and that many members of the crowd surged forward to dip their kerchiefs in the royal blood, either as a protection against the king's evil (a.k.a. scrofula: *"le roy te touche, Dieu te guerisse"* – "the king touches you, God cures you" – it is known, for instance, that Charles II, Charles's son, touched 92,107 persons in one year for similar reasons), or in a desire to bear witness to something that felt inherently (i.e. instinctively, as opposed to logically) wrong.

Nostradamus was not, however, merely interested in the doings of the great men and women of history – the movers and the shakers, the kings and the queens, the politicians and the tyrants – to the exclusion of all others. He also turned his attention towards smaller events – just as crucial to those who experienced them, of course, but in real danger of being left out of history altogether, thanks to the illiteracy and powerlessness of many of those who experienced them. Nostradamus attempts to rectify the situation in quatrains like this:

Witchcraft at Carcassonne

DATE 1571, CENTURY IX, QUATRAIN 71

"Au lieux sacrez animaux veu à trixe,
Avec celuy qui n'osera le iour:
A Carcassonne pour disgrace propice,
Sera posé pour plus ample seiour."

At the sacred place animals are seen with the croton
Alongside he who does not dare the day
A much-needed disgrace at Carcassonne
Will settle in for a longer stay.

The "croton" is the castor-oil plant (known, according to Book V of Dioscorides's 1st-century AD *Materia Medica*, as *trixis* – thus Nostradamus's *trixe*), and renowned for irritating the skin and causing tumours – this ties in with "he who does not dare the day", for it is of the devil and his Luciferan followers that we are talking, and the sacred grove clearly belongs to them (the Luciferans, who rejected both Catholicism and Catharism, even conducted underground orgies, believing that activities carried out underground were somehow more permissible). Euphonically, the word *trixe* also has phallic connotations, as in *trique*, which means a penis or a baton to hit people with (and in its written form, to have an erection), and this ties in with devil-worship too, for we know that the Luciferans frequently used penis-substitutes and phallic objects in their rites. We also know that the Inquisition, during its investigations into witchcraft, would use both croton oil and belladonna to torment its often innocent victims. Sticking to Nostradamus's diabolically euphonic line, therefore, we also find the *strix* or *striga*, a nocturnal Roman bird of ill omen which ate human flesh and, in particular, the flesh of children purportedly conceived in diabolical ceremonies – its legend survived well into the Middle Ages, as delineated in Isidore's *Etymologiae* – a famous example of such alleged paedophagy (cannibalism conducted on children) occurred at Orléans, well within Nostradamus's lifetime. We are speaking of witchcraft in Carcassonne, therefore, which together with Toulouse was considered, in medieval times, to be the most bedevilled part of Europe outside Austria and the Savoy. Nostradamus's index date of 71 then takes us directly to 1571, which proved to be something of a bumper year for witchcraft trials in France – a magician pseudonymously called *Trois-Echelles* (Three Ladders), for instance, was executed in Paris that same year after somewhat unwisely claiming that there were upwards of 100,000 witches operating throughout the length and breadth of the country.

Would you like another example? Let's take an even more esoteric one this time. One that will demonstrate the full breadth of Nostradamus's geographical and historical reach, and also his sense of humour – something most previous commentators seem to have left out of their computations altogether.

Ibrahim the Mad

DATE 1640, CENTURY I, QUATRAIN 40

"La trombe faulse dissimulant folie
Fera Bizance un changement de loys:
Hystra d'Egypte qui veult que l'on deslie,
Edict changeant monnoyes & aloys."

The fake waterspout conceals madness
It will trigger a change of the law in Byzantium
The hysteric of Egypt who wishes to be thought acute
An edict changes coin into fish.

Read on – you won't regret it! This is one of Nostradamus's most fantastical and extraordinary quatrains, with puns galore. First, definitions. *"Trombe"* is not a trumpet, as many commentators have falsely supposed, but a "waterspout", and *"hystra"* comes from *hystérie* (although *hystrix*, in Latin, can mean a porcupine – also, of course, a fish, in the sense of an *hérisson de mer*, ergo a porcupine fish). *"Deslie"*, too, is often mistranslated, and actually comes from *délié*, meaning "acute" or sharp (the opposite of "madness" and "hysteria"), and *"aloys"*, finally, comes from the *alose*, a large fish caught in the Seine during the spring season. However, there are two more puns on "coins" and "alloys" hidden within the quatrain, for *loi* (*loy*) is an alternative spelling of the Old French word *aloi* (archaic spelling *aloy*) meaning alloy, with both used in terms of *monnayage* (coining). This leaves us with a seemingly rather dotty quatrain, although all Nostradamus's talk of madness and hysteria has somewhat prepared us for it – the parallel reading for line two, for example, would give

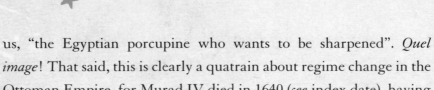

us, "the Egyptian porcupine who wants to be sharpened". *Quel image*! That said, this is clearly a quatrain about regime change in the Ottoman Empire, for Murad IV died in 1640 (*see* index date), having inherited the sultanate from a "mad" uncle, the neurotic Mustafa I. He then bequeathed it to an even "madder" brother, Ibrahim, whom he belatedly ordered, from his deathbed, to be executed, fearing that Ibrahim would only botch the reign. The orders were not carried out, and the neurasthenic and clinically depressed Ibrahim did indeed botch the reign, bringing the Ottoman Empire perilously close to dissolution in a little under eight years. And now for Nostradamus's *pièce de résistance* – Ibrahim was discovered one day "feeding coins to fish" (*see* line four), an activity that led to his being given the nickname, "Ibrahim the Mad". But that's not all. The "waterspout" in line one is another magnificent stroke, for Ibrahim, who collected very fat women, decided, on a whim, to drown all 280 houris in his harem by throwing them into the communal pool in order to create a tremendous splash. When he heard about Ibrahim's intentions, the Grand Mufti decided that enough was enough, and he arranged for Ibrahim to be quietly disposed of in a palace coup.

I think you'll agree that these quatrains hold up in every respect, up to and including that of the index date. Here's one final, exquisite example, which I couldn't resist including – the index date is a little problematic, true, but then again, the poet responsible for the "famous myth" in line 4 *was* born in 1641:

The Song of La Palisse

DATE 1716, CENTURY X, QUATRAIN 41

"En la frontiere de Caussade et Charlus,
Non guieres loing du fonds de la vallee,
De ville franche musicque à son de luths,
Environnez combouls et grand myttee."

On the border between Caussade and Charlus
Not very far from the valley estate
Lute music will sound from the free city [Villefranche]
Incorporating cymbals and a famous myth.

Jacques II de Chabannes, Lord of la Palice, Chevalier, Baron de Curton et de Rochefort, Seigneur de Caussade (*see* quatrain), Madic, Charlus (*see* quatrain), la Dailhe, Aurires, Solon-la-Gane, Saignes, la Roche-Machalin and Tinires, was made Grand Master of France in 1511, and later Marshall, under François I. La Palice was known for his valour, and for his desire always to be at the forefront in any combat. Despite being taken prisoner for a second time at Guinegate in 1513, he escaped, and took part in the capture of "Villefranche" (*see* quatrain) and in the Battle of Marignan. He was killed, in 1525, at the famous Battle of Pavia, considered by many to be the first great modern battle, and in which canoneers replaced knights for the very first time, resulting in the virtual annihilation of the standing French army. And that, in normal circumstances, would have been that. But one curious thing emerges from the fog of battle, and it relates rather nicely to Nostradamus's otherwise elusive quatrain – la Palice's soldiers composed a song about him. The song, in its original form, went: "*Hélas, s'il n'était pas mort, il ferait encore envie*" – "Alas, if he wasn't dead, they would still be envying him." Now in Old French (and as with Nostradamus), esses and effs may sometimes be printed or written to look exactly like one another – most times, when this happens, the meaning is obvious from the context, but in the case of la Palice's song, serendipity has it that were the ess to be mistaken for the eff, it would create a meaning so sublime in its tautological illogic that it was inevitable that, somewhere along the line, a poet with a humorous streak should pick it up and run with it. The poet in question was Bernard de la Monnoye (1641 [*see* index date]–1728), and he read the original French as "*Hélas, s'il n'était pas mort, il serait encore en vie*" – "Alas, if he wasn't dead, he would still be alive." Galvanized by this happy occurrence, de la Monnoye set to work. First, he coined the neologism "*lapalissade*", meaning an utterly obvious truth, or truism. Not content with this achievement, however, the French Academician went on to write a truly catchy song to cement his discovery, which he entitled the *Chanson de la Palisse*. Here's a taster:

Monsieur d'la Palisse est mort,	Monsieur de la Palice is dead
il est mort devant Pavie,	He died before Pavie
Un quart d'heure avant sa mort,	A quarter of an hour earlier
il était encore en vie.	He was still alive
Il fut par un triste sort	By a sad twist of fate
blessé d'une main cruelle,	He was wounded by a cruel hand
On croit, puisqu'il en est mort,	One assumes (because he died of it)
que la plaie était mortelle.	That the wound was a mortal one.
Regretté de ses soldats,	Lamented by his men
il mourut digne d'envie,	He died an enviable death
Et le jour de son trépas	The day he died
fut le dernier de sa vie.	Was his last
Il mourut le vendredi,	His death occurred on a Friday
le dernier jour de son âge,	The last day he would age
S'il fût mort le samedi,	If it had been a Saturday
il eût vécu davantage.	He would have lived even longer.

The four examples I have chosen for you in this foreword are as disparate a bunch of verses as it is surely possible to contrive. But that's exactly why I chose them. For they illustrate, between them, the differing, but still analogous, aspects of Nostradamus's genius — that of the historian, the philosopher, the iconoclast, the comedian, the futurologist, and, yes, the seer.

INTRODUCTION

I believe that I can fairly claim to be the only exegetist in the more than 450-year history of Nostradamus scholarship who has ever thought to ask themselves whether the seer's own index dates – I'm referring to the numbers 1 to 100 that accompany each of the ten *Centuries* inside which he ordered his 942 extant quatrains (*see* Foreword) – are actually accurate. This is hardly surprising, as it's not the sort of question one can answer for oneself in a few casual sittings.

It had struck me very early on in my enquiries that it would be hard to argue a rational case for Nostradamus's choice of the *Century* (that is, for the 10 separate periods of 100 years that he chose as his fundamental index definition) to be an entirely random one. No, when Nostradamus says a hundred he has to mean it, and the expedient and seemingly wilful avoidance of this fact by generations of his commentators (presumably because it's a darn sight easier to draw from a 700-year potential strike pool than a 7-year one) still bewilders me.

Other commentators have translated the quatrains, and then trawled through all of (largely Western) history to find an expedient, random match. I have translated the quatrains and have then trawled through all of world history, checking, as a first resort, each possible year out of a grand total of seven, until I have come across an exact correlation, referred to by at least three separate points in the quatrain text, and which could not reasonably apply to any other era. When I say seven possible years, I mean, for instance, 1480, 1580, 1680, 1780, 1880, 1980 or 2080, for an index date of 80, for I now believe that Nostradamus, who was obsessed by the number 7 – he mentions the number more than 50 times within 942 quatrains, and finished up with a quatrain in which 7 is mentioned as the "great number" following "whose completion" the world will end – quite consciously decided on a 700-year window (with a 7,000-year extension in terms of Armageddon) for his quatrains.

Nostradamus is not alone, of course, in imbuing the number 7 with exceptional significance, for 7 has long been considered a holy number. The moon, for instance, has seven phases, just as there are seven bodies in alchemy, seven senses, seven deadly sins, seven virtues, and seven spirits before the throne of God. There were seven days in creation, seven graces, seven days needed for Levitical purification, seven days in the week, seven wise masters, and seven great champions of Christendom. There are seven divisions in the Lord's Prayer, seven ages in the life of man, seven "falls" each day by the just, each seventh year is deemed sabbatical, and seven-times-seven years is taken to represent a jubilee. Seven weeks demarcated the first two of the great three Jewish feasts, each of which lasted for seven days, just as there are seven churches of Asia, seven candlesticks, seven trumpets, seven stars, seven horns, seven eyes attributed to the Lamb of God, ten-times-seven Israelites on the move to Egypt, who were then exiled for seven years, and who lived under the nominal guidance of ten-times-seven elders. There are, in addition, seven bibles or sacred books (the Christian Bible, the Scandinavian Eddas, the Five Kings of the Chinese, the Mohammedan Koran, the Buddhist Tri Pitikes, the three Vedas of the Hindus, and the Persian Zend-Avesta), seven joys and seven sorrows of the Virgin, seven chakras in Hindu kundalini, seven brothers of the Mayan Father Sun and seven Mayan corporeal power centres, seven sages of Greece, and even, dare one say it, seven wonders of the ancient world.

I have only cast my net wider than Nostradamus's 700-year cycle when absolutely no accurate index date has seemed to fit the bill, or when a quatrain seemed, at first glance, to fail. For I now believe that Nostradamus, like the Mayan Chilans before him, understood that time was not linear (i.e. that it did not move inexorably forwards, mimicking the birth-to-grave progress of the human body), but that it worked spirally, interleaving past with present, and affording those who were marked by God – or those who, like the Mayan Masters of Time, had either inherited, achieved through self-sacrifice, or otherwise honed their spiritual intuition such that they had become carriers of the Eternal Wisdom – the ability to see, albeit briefly, the past as not merely the past, but also as a forward echo of both the present and the future.

Continuing with the spiral analogy, Nostradamus was therefore able, like the Chilans, to gain brief glimpses (at the – shall we call it? – turn of the spiral) into an ever-present, eternally repetitive, but nevertheless eternally changing cosmic cycle. My task was therefore to allow readers, for the very first time in history, to monitor the full panoply of Nostradamus's projections into our past, present, and future world, without the drag anchor of ancient prejudice.

I first began to follow up my hunch about the index dates in 2005, when I was writing my *Nostradamus: The Complete Prophecies for the Future*. I then took my hunch one step further, in 2006, when I was writing my *Nostradamus: The Good News*. Thanks to the runaway success of those two experiments, I decided to try for the Full Monty with my *The Complete Prophecies of Nostradamus*. During the year the book took me to research and write, it rapidly became clear that I was approaching a breakthrough of major significance – something that would quite conceivably turn Nostradamus scholarship around on its head. My final tally for the *Complete Nostradamus* came out at 815 out of a total of 942 quatrains in which the index date specifically matched a numerologically analogous year. An incredible total, surely, and one which any future Nostradamus commentator must ignore at their peril.

The self-imposed scrupulousness dictated by the premise of accurate index dates made my task considerably more difficult than it might otherwise have been, but it also repaid me magnificently, in the sense that it opened up a plethora of new readings which reinforced in my mind (and, I hope, in my readers' minds) the sheer jaw-dropping brilliance of Nostradamus's powers of precognition. It is simply too much of a stretch to believe that the awesome number of quatrains which are perfect in both date and fact can possibly have arisen as the result of some weird form of serendipity (akin to those typewriting monkeys who will eventually – or so we are reliably informed – succeed in recreating the Bible word for word if they rattle away for long enough).

I should perhaps come clean now and say that people anticipating a simple rehash of previous famous predictions in my author's choice of the top 100 are going to be seriously disappointed, for I have approached each quatrain with entirely fresh eyes, and translated it without any recourse to either earlier translations or to erstwhile set-in-stone interpretations. To achieve this end I have occasionally used a technique of my own invention which I call "euphonic translation". This technique takes into account the crucial importance, whilst translating Nostradamus, of bearing in mind the actual *sound* of the line (alongside its more literal, conventional interpretation, needless to say), together with the often hidden meanings and *jeux d'esprits* potentially contained within those sounds. Many commentators have never cottoned on to this possibility (despite French being the euphonic language that it is!) and have therefore restricted themselves slavishly to the written and often misprinted text – they are thinking purely linearly, in other words. This often limits access to possible meanings which should, and in my opinion, do, inform the whole. The proof, of course, is in the pudding.

In some cases, where either or all possible meanings (the literal, the metaphorical, and the codified) may need to be taken into account, I have put the second, subsidiary (or non-linear) meaning in brackets. A good example occurs in 10/89 – 1789: The French Revolution – it comes in line three, with the word *Laqueduict*. The word may be taken literally, as a misprinting for *L'Aqueduct* (an aqueduct), or it may be taken euphonically as *Là qu'eux dit* (literally, "that which was said, by them, there"). In my view Nostradamus often signals such bilateral readings by the purposeful misspelling of an obvious word, or its inclusion in a place where its objective reading makes no sense whatsoever (whereas its euphonic reading does). He can then rely on the tunnel vision common to most scholars – i.e. that there must be a literal answer to everything, or the world cannot possibly make sense – to protect his hidden meanings. I, on the other hand, am neither a scholar, and nor do I feel that the world necessarily needs to make sense (I believe in God – *He* makes sense). I therefore hold no truck whatsoever with such unnecessary and crippling limitations. As a (hopefully enlightened) commentator I am simply out to get as close to Nostradamus's core meaning as possible, and if that involves a few unforced errors, well then, so be it – I beg the forgiveness of my readers.

Such techniques have led me to a series of extraordinary discoveries which would not have been possible if I had not chosen to take this somewhat unconventional approach. Without recourse to euphonic translation and the acceptance of Nostradamus's own index numbers, for instance, I would never have discovered 8/69: Antonio Stradivari (1669), or 1/95: J.S. Bach (1695). Quatrain 10/4: Battle of Blenheim (1704) would have made no sense whatsoever, and I might have assumed that 1/76: American Declaration of Independence (1776) referred simply to Napoleon Bonaparte, as generations of commentators have chosen to believe before me. I challenge anyone, however, to read my radically new interpretations of the text and not to, at the very least, admit to a tentative reconsideration of their former position.

As far as my source materials are concerned, I have invariably gone for the earliest possible printed versions of the quatrains, on the assumption that the earlier the better, as far as unforced printing errors are concerned – later printed books often compounded earlier errors by falsely assuming that they were correct and then further adapting their content to fit the previous blooper. I have therefore checked my French texts meticulously against all the remaining original printings (i.e. the Bonhomme "Lyon", the "Utrecht" Du Rosne "Lyon", the Du Rosne "Lyon" itself, and the Benoist Rigaud "Lyon") and have indicated, in brackets, where there are disparities between the different editions that might afford a potentially different reading.

I have also, as mentioned in my previous books, taken particular care in my renditions of the classical references and mythologies in Nostradamus's writings – for Nostradamus would, like any educated person in 16th-century France, have had a vast body of classical learning at his fingertips, and would have considered its use, and his readers' understanding of classical myth, as a *sine qua non*. A similar wellhead of knowledge needs to be used when interpreting the quatrains today, and negates any half-baked ideas that Nostradamus wrote in a secret or Green Language, accessible only to privileged initiates, or to those versed in the secret lore of the Akashic Chronicle. He was, quite simply, extremely well read and well educated.

The key to Nostradamus, in my opinion, lies in the actual process of translation – the act of translating opens the commentator's mind to what Nostradamus, through the centuries (both literally and metaphorically), is trying to tell him. It becomes a dialogue, in other words, with Nostradamus as the guiding hand in the discussion. The commentator must therefore approach each of the quatrains with an open mind, and with the capacity to be surprised in a serendipitous manner. For I now believe that what the seer intended was nothing short of a complete history of the past, present, and future *as he saw it*. For during the lengthy process of translation and commentary, Nostradamus's quatrains, buoyed by the accuracy of his index dates, slowly formed themselves before my eyes into a wave of knowledge which spanned a period from the classical world, through the birth of Christ, to the end of the world and Armageddon.

I trust that, when you read the commentaries which follow, you will feel that I have achieved my task of opening up Nostradamus's work to the public's critical gaze. And that the 100 key quatrains I have chosen for this book effectively demonstrate the full supra-national panoply of Nostradamus's quite extraordinary breadth of historical reference.

BIOGRAPHICAL PREAMBLE

The idea that any historian or biographer is "right", or is creating more than yet another believable and interesting myth to overlay and influence an already existing myth, is fundamentally absurd. Few people can even describe the day that has just passed accurately — let alone decades, if not centuries, before their own time. No, what historians and biographers are giving us is an informed opinion, and a vastly subjective one at that, dependent on the often sparse material that has been left, frequently as a result of random historical happenstance, and to which they inevitably ascribe — because they have a vested interest in so doing — far too much significance.

The winners in history customarily hide what is inconvenient to them, or manipulate the truth to suit the scale of their ambitions, and the losers bleat, or are written out of history altogether (Mithraism being one obvious example) — that is, after all, human nature. When losers do out-survive those they feel have done them (or their cabal) wrong, as often as not they try to rewrite history the better to reinforce their feelings of outrage and despair – that too is human nature. All history is therefore fiction disguised as fact, but actually representing the historians' best shot at an almost-truth. It is for exactly this reason that apocryphal stories, hearsay, and scandal are potentially just as historically relevant as (purported) dry facts, government documents (a likely story), and contemporary commentaries (untarnished, of course, by even the merest hint of vainglory or rodomontade!).

Wars have been fought over lesser issues than the details of Nostradamus's alleged biography. Scholars have been declaring that only they know the true story from as far back as the late 16th century, and their descendants still continue to do so today (and with equal impunity). So little is actually known about Nostradamus's life, however, that some of the more apocryphal stories, often stemming from a century or so after his death, become important pointers in themselves – not so much to the "real life" (as if anyone is capable of teasing that out from the mass of obfuscation, forgery, and hearsay that underlies much Nostradamus scholarship) as to the life he ought to have led, given the reality of his influence.

Anyway, here is a short biographical note that does not purport to be the exact truth (what can?) so much as to coalesce both given, disputed, and established facts into some sort of sensible (if inevitably fallible) order.

BIOGRAPHICAL NOTE

The medieval France *Profonde* (i.e. distanced, both culturally and geographically from Paris) into which Michel de Nostredame (1503–66) was born, encompassed a mass of different sects, tribes, and communities, but with no truly effective central government. Villagers from the Pyrenees or from deepest Provence, for instance, might never even have heard of Paris, nor would they have understood Parisian French if it were spoken to them – faces, manners, and even language varied alarmingly according to the contours of the valleys in which people lived.

Isolated communities were surrounded by a ripple-effect of further enclaves, mini-fiefdoms, clan centres (with bells delineating tribal territories), and racial diversifications, dating all the way back to pre-history – a charivari that remained in place well into the 19th century, with distant echoes of its dying fall still reverberating today.

Few French people had ever seen a map of France. Fewer still were aware of French history as a definable, ongoing process. Of the total population, 98 per cent were deemed to be Catholic, it is true, but with marked variations in religious practice. Local priests competed with quacks, witches, healers, simple-mongers, and weather merchants for the hearts and souls of their parish. Before the French Revolution (1789–99), the word "France" was merely used to describe a truncated area in and around Paris. In Provence, someone from the north might be termed a *Franciot* or *Franchiman*, and the Provençal-born and Francoprovençal-speaking Nostradamus would most probably have grown up with a quasi-atavistic mistrust of both the royal government and its motivations (largely on account of a cultural and linguistic bifurcation that was only really addressed by the Abbé Henri Grégoire at the time of the 1793–94 Reign of Terror).

For Nostradamus, it must be remembered, was both a committed, mainstream Catholic, and an ethnic – and therefore potentially ostracizable – Jew. If that sounds like a paradox, it wasn't perceived as such in a 16th-century France dedicated to both God, in the form of the Inquisition, and mammon, in the form of the pillaging of others' property for reasons of ecclesiastical expediency. For 30 years, under the reign of Good King René, the Jews of Provence had been accorded the free practice of their religion, but all that ended with René's death in 1480, a date which unfortunately coincided with the inception of the Spanish Inquisition.

By the time of Nostradamus's birth in 1503, most prominent Jews had prudently converted to a pragmatic form of Catholicism, thanks to the edicts of, respectively, Charles VIII in 1488, and Louis XII in 1501. This didn't prevent the French Crown from occasionally plundering their possessions, but it did offer them a measure of protection in a country suddenly rife with religious intolerance and paranoia. So the infant Michel de Nostredame found himself both uncircumcised (the penalty for which, under Levitical law, is ostracism from the congregation of Israel), and baptized according to the Christian rite, whilst retaining, in the form of his maternal great-grandfather, Jean de Saint-Rémy, an intimate access to the Jewish chain of tradition, the *Schalscheleth Ha-Kabbalah*, which was to stand him in very good stead in his later incarnation as a diviner and scryer.

As a result of this upbringing, Nostradamus almost certainly dabbled in magic, and very certainly in mysticism and the kabbalah, which encapsulated the Jewish search for new wisdom in a creative synthesis between the mythologies of ancient Egypt, ancient Greece, Assyrian astrology, Babylonian magic, Arabian divination, Platonic philosophy, and Gnosticism (Gershom Scholem in his *Major Trends in Jewish Mysticism* writes that "it can be taken as certain that…ancient writings, with Gnostic excerpts written in Hebrew, made their way from the East to Provence…to become one of the chief influences which shaped the theosophy of the 13th-century kabbalists").

The secretive and mystical nature of the kabbalah, therefore, would have provided a much-needed escape from the grim realities of Jewish life in an Inquisitorial Europe, and a much-needed panacea in the face of the forcible conversions that followed René's death. By pure chance, Nostradamus's native town of St-Rémy was the perfect place to study the kabbalah, as Provence was generally acknowledged as home to the earliest kabbalistic community in France. Paradoxically, perhaps, Nostradamus, as well as being a kabbalist, an alchemist, and a Talmudist, was also a fervent adherent to Catholic doctrine throughout his life, and would certainly not have been accepted at Avignon University (not then a part of France) had he not been sincere in these assertions, and in his excoriation of the near ubiquitous Lutheran heresy. He later enrolled, again without problem, at the venerable University of Montpellier (founded in 1220) in order to study medicine – a wise move, as Montpellier possessed, without doubt, the greatest school of medicine of those times.

After matriculating from Montpellier (from which he had briefly been expelled on 3 October 1529, for the alleged crime of having practised as an apothecary, before being readmitted, third time lucky, on 23 October that same year) – and following hard upon an invigilation process that would have been conducted in the medieval manner of a formal dispute between the student and the teaching staff, rather than merely by written examination – Nostradamus was plunged straight into the treatment of an outbreak of the plague.

Encumbered by the usual paraphernalia worn by medical practitioners during such crises (Irish physician Neil O'Glacan (1590–1655), in his *Tractatus de Peste* (Toulouse 1629), describes plague doctors as wearing long leather gowns stained with many different coloured powders, gauntlets, leather masks with glass protection for the eyes, and a long sponge-filled beak imbrued with fumigants for the nose), Nostradamus struck out into entirely new territory with his invention of a purifying powder (his "rose pill"), which, we are led to believe, inspired an entirely untypical confidence in his patients. As a direct consequence of this experience, Nostradamus became something of an authority on the plague, a talent that was sorely tested when plague struck, once again, during his tenure as a doctor at Agen, killing his young wife and their two children. As a result, Nostradamus not only suffered from the usual criticism of "Physician, heal thyself", but was also sued by the distraught family of his wife for the return of her dowry.

Traumatized by his loss, Nostradamus took to the road, and travelled through many parts of France, Italy, and Sicily, before finally settling in Salon de Provence. There, at the age of 44, he met a widow, Anne Ponsarde Gemelle (*gemellus* implies a twin in Latin), whom he married on 11 November 1547. They moved into a house on the Rue Ferreiraux (now known as Rue Nostradamus), and Nostradamus, in considerable demand by this time, not least for his sovereign remedies, continued his travels.

It was during this period that, thanks to his meetings with apothecaries, physicians, and magicians, he first began to suspect that he had the gift of prophecy and second sight. He was not the only one. Under the reign of the 13 Valois kings, it was estimated that there were upwards of 30,000 astrologers, sorcerers, alchemists, and prophets practising in Paris alone, and it is to Nostradamus's credit, and to that of his art, that he rose, inexorably, to the top of a very crowded tree.

Three years after the publication of his *Traité des Fardemens* in 1552 (an *à la mode* treatise on unguents, jams, and preserves of all kinds), Nostradamus followed up – rather tentatively, it must be said – with the first edition of his famous *Centuries* (1555), fearing, according to his pupil, Jean Aymes de Chavigny, both castigation and mockery. The 353 quatrains, to just about everybody's surprise, including that of Nostradamus, were a sensation. Summoned to Paris by Henri II's queen, Catherine de Medici, barely a year after publication, Nostradamus returned to Salon a rich man, having discovered, the hard way, that private practice (the casting of personal horoscopes and the alleviation of courtiers' ailments) was considerably more remunerative, and a good deal less precarious, than celebrity stargazing. Nostradamus continued to advise the queen, however, not least because she protected him, in some measure, from falling foul of the religious authorities for blasphemy, while her regal favour afforded him a much-appreciated kudos and the promise of a steady income.

Nostradamus's career really took off with his extraordinary series of quatrains depicting the accidental death, in a joust, of King Henri II of France. This uncannily accurate series of five quatrains cemented Nostradamus's reputation with Catherine de Medici, and ensured him an uninterrupted income stream from enthusiastic clients for the rest of his life.

In a rare but salutary bout of discretion, Nostradamus disguised the true dates of the king's death, knowing that regicide – or even the suspicion of regicide – carried an exemplary and excruciating series of publicly witnessed tortures. The fact that Nostradamus's fears for the king's life were seconded by Luca Gaurico, the court astrologer, afforded him further credence. That they were also convenient to the queen, who wished to prevent her husband from following certain courses of action she found uncongenial, merely served to endear Nostradamus further to her heart.

In terms of the apparent dangers Nostradamus faced from the Inquisition, it is important to draw a distinction, just as Alexander of Hales (1183–1245) did, between the two principal, although different, forms of magic. Namely *divination* (from the Latin *divinitas*, meaning the godhead, or the divine nature), which was seen as High Magic; and *maleficum* or evil-doing (from the Latin *maleficus*, meaning hurtful or mischievous), which, in the Middle Ages, was the word coined to represent Low Magic. Low Magic was designed for instant gratification – the equivalent, in magical terms, of a caffeine hit. It might span the ritual burning of hair, the spearing of wax dolls, or sacrificial offerings leading to fruitful crops or the emergence of rain after a long dry spell. High Magic incorporated astrology and alchemy, and was built on a firm philosophical foundation, deriving as much from Pythagoras as it did from the Persian Magi, Gnosticism, or Neo-Platonism. Both were thus categorically different in origin, with Low Magic drawing much of its motive power from Aristotelianism. High Magic was therefore a subject of justifiable study, and if not quite "nice", at least intellectually acceptable. Low Magic was considered akin to witchcraft.

Nostradamus, needless to say, was a High Magic figure, taking his cue from the *Corpus Hermeticum*, a magical treatise believed, in medieval times, to be of the highest antiquity, but later proved by Isaac Casaubon (no relation, beyond the obvious, to George Eliot's fictional *Middlemarch* antihero) to have been composed circa the 2nd or 3rd century AD – Casaubon's opinion carried great weight, as, in his day (1559–1614) he was considered, alongside the Agen-born Joseph Scaliger, to be the most learned man in Europe.

Nostradamus's adherence to High Magic, therefore, provided him with considerable protection from Inquisitorial inquiry, and, alongside his support from the queen, made it even more likely that he did not have either the need or the motivation to hide or codify his index dates (except in the aforementioned extreme circumstances, when they dealt with the death of living kings). This High Magic itinerary of Nostradamus's also tallies with his pedagogical intentions – for he truly believed that mankind was subject to an overweening fate, and that nothing in history occurred as the result of accident. Everything was either intended or preprogrammed, and as such could be teased out through scrying, divination, necromancy, hydromancy, chiromancy, astrology, dream interpretation, the study of ancient texts, numerology, alchemy, the kabbalah, hermetic inference, and the manipulation of the fundamental chemical composition of inanimate objects. With each step in the divinatory cycle, the adept was led to a higher level of understanding, which culminated in a process of mental and spiritual purification leading to absolute clarity of thought. Such a spiritual catharsis allowed the adept access to hidden truths that, with the best possible of intentions, he would then lay before the world to make of it what it willed.

Such apparent self-glorification was frowned on by the religious community, but it wasn't, for the most part, considered witchcraft, and its zealots were allowed to practise, to all intents and purposes, unmolested. However, magic was, most definitely, anti-clerical, in the sense that many of its adherents believed that they had been specifically chosen to express God's intentions, rather than simply to respond to them, as a priest or a true believer would. To this extent alone was Nostradamus in danger, and he retorted to such allegations by making it clear, on numerous occasions, that he did not feel himself to be a consciously chosen vessel, but merely a random one, selected by happenstance.

Consciously chosen vessel or not, the summit of Nostradamus's stratospherical celebrity career came during a royal visit to Salon itself, in 1564, by the boy king, Charles IX (who would later, at his dominant mother's instigation, approve the St Bartholomew's Day Massacre). Catherine invited Nostradamus and his family to a private visit at the royal apartments, and then to a further consultation, where she asked him to cast the horoscope of her youngest son, the Duke of Anjou. Nostradamus was more interested in the young Henri de Navarre, however, and even investigated the ten-year-old child whilst he was sleeping, predicting that he would eventually inherit all of France.

Thanks to the evidence contained in Nostradamus's last will and testament, we know that he must have been very well paid for his troubles, a factor that must have provided him with considerable comfort during his declining years, for, assailed by gout, arthritis, and a heart condition that even his own sovereign remedies failed to alleviate, he finally succumbed on 2 July 1566, in exactly the fashion he had predicted for himself.

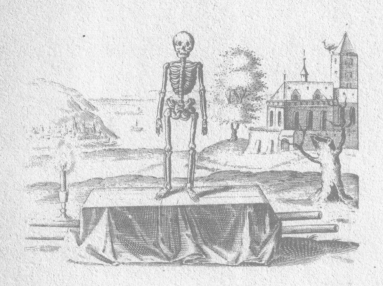

NOSTRADAMUS'S DIVINATORY TECHNIQUE

IN HIS OWN WORDS

It would be far too simple a trick to trawl through the numerous works by the plethora of self-proclaimed alchemists, diviners, seers, scryers, soothsayers, clairvoyants, augurs, sibyls, futurists, presagers, prognosticators and sages which make up the mediaeval eschatological "bestiary", and tease out a few well-known prophetic techniques, before larding these onto Nostradamus as if by default.

Fortunately, the man himself wrote a number of highly personal and detailed quatrains describing the techniques he used and the philosophy inherent in his actions. I therefore append these here (*see* pages 40–3), for my readers' benefit, and to ensure that when they read the prophecies, they take with them a suitable image of the man who – when all is said and done – actually wrote them.

Nostradamus Explains His Technique

DATE 1555, CENTURY I, QUATRAIN 1

"Etant assis de nuit secret estude,
Seul repousé sus la selle d'aerain,
Flambe exigue sortant de solitude,
Fait proferer qui n'est à croire vain."

Finally seated, at night, in secret study
At rest and alone over the bronze stool
A slender flame emerges from the wilderness
Unbelievable deeds are uttered from the wasteland.

What is interesting about this quatrain is the position Nostradamus accords himself when divining – "over" the bronze stool or tripod. This correlates with what we have heard about his divining techniques, namely that after preparing himself with spiritual exercises and copious amounts of hallucination-enhancing nutmeg, he would stoop over a bowl of ink-stained water, a cloth spread about his head to avoid residual light, and then, by means of meditation, enter a trance-like state, becoming possessed by what he called the "spirits of the void" (it is instructive to note here that in the Old French, "*solitude*", in line three, and "*vain*", in line four, mean a wasteland, a waste, a wilderness, or a void, and not "solitude" or "vain", as many translators have wrongly supposed).

Nostradamus probably adapted his technique from that expounded by the 4th-century Syrian Neo-Platonist philosopher and student of Porphyry Malchus, Iamblicus Chalcidensis, in his treatise, the *Theurgia*, or *De Mysteriis Aegyptiorum*, which was reprinted in Lyon in 1547 by the same house that printed many of Nostradamus's later works. Iamblicus speaks of the divining methods used by the Persian Zoroastrian priests, or Magi, in an effort to interpret and influence the battle between darkness and light (*aša*/the truth and *druj*/the lie). This eternal struggle would also have been much on Nostradamus's mind as he attempted to see into the wastes, and to influence future behaviour for the benefit of humanity.

The use of "bronze" in line two, is also of interest here, as it was considered a key alchemical element, as well as being a better conductor than either steel or iron. Such things were seen in strongly symbolical terms by Nostradamus, and may well have influenced his choice of bronze as a settle.

Entering a Trance

DATE 1555, CENTURY I, QUATRAIN 2

"La verge en maï mise au milieu de BRANCHES
De l'onde il moulle & le limbe & le pied.
Un peur & voix fremissent par les manches,
Splendeur divine. Le divin prés s'assied."

The hawthorn rod is placed at the centre of the tripod
He wets both his limbs and his feet with the wavelets
Frightened, and with a trembling voice
Divine splendour. God is near. He sits.

When taken with 1/1 – 1555: Nostradamus Explains his Technique, what we are given is a pretty clear picture of the sort of ritual Nostradamus went through before essaying a connection with what he called the "void" or "wasteland". The mention of the hawthorn rod (*la verge en maï*) is of particular interest here, as the Romans considered hawthorn a charm against sorcery and lightning, and were wont to place leaves from its branches across the cots of newly born children (hawthorn being sacred to the Roman goddess Maia Maiestas). There is also a connection between the word *maï*, the French word *magi* (magic) and the Magi, suggested in the previous quatrain, as all the words arguably come from the same root, namely the Latin *maius/Magius*, which corresponds to the Sanskrit word *mah*, meaning to "grow". Hawthorn, in addition, is often used for dowsing, as it responds well to water (being traditionally connected to holy wells), and this direction-seeking aspect is doubtless why Nostradamus places the stick at the exact centre of the water-filled tripod.

Alchemy

DATE 1555, CENTURY III, QUATRAIN 2

"Le divin verbe donrra à la sustance
Comprins ciel, terre, or occult au faict mystique
Corps, ame, esprit aiant toute puissance,
Tant sous ses pieds, comme au siege celique."

The word of God will give to the substance
Which comprises heaven, earth, and the alchemist's golden secret
A body, soul, and spirit of all-consuming power
On Earth and in Hell, just as in Heaven's seat.

Nostradamus is describing the Great Void here, a term representing the alchemical euphemism for the fundamental "ground of the being", and one, in addition, that finds itself spontaneously contained within memory, in the form of the "collective unconscious". In that sense the Void could be said to correspond to a blank slate awaiting mystic revelation. Nostradamus makes it very clear in these three great explanatory quatrains that when he enters one of his scrying trances, he feels that he is connecting with this Void or Wasteland, and that it is inhabiting him – and he, it – in the form of an Hermetic identity. That what may seem divine revelation is in fact a chemical/mystical occurrence triggered through the placing of the tree of knowledge (in the symbolical form of a hawthorn branch) into the exact centre of the divine elixir (a.k.a. the water of life), this time in the symbolical form of a darkened water bowl. This sacred marriage of Spirit and Materia was to form the basis of Nostradamus's divinatory powers.

PRINCES, PRESIDENTS and PLUNDERERS

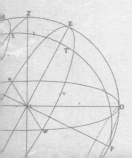

Philip II of Spain

DATE 1589, CENTURY IX, QUATRAIN 89

"Sept ans sera Philip. fortune prospere,
Rabaissera des Arabes l'effaict,
Puis son mydi perplex rebors affaire
Ieusne ongyon abysmera son sort."

For seven years Philip's fortunes will prosper
He will reduce the Arab army
Then, halfway through, things will perplexingly turn against him
A young onion will destroy his future.

The index date of 89 and the content of this quatrain lead us directly to King Philip II of Spain (1527–98). After a very shaky start, when Spain suffered from massive inflation and Philip's obsession with sheep farming forced the country to become a net importer of food, Philip moved into a golden period, in which Spain blossomed. This period came to a sudden end with the execution of Mary, Queen of Scots, in 1587, and was further exacerbated by the many armadas Philip sent to England in consequence – all of which failed. As a result, Philip went bankrupt (for the fourth time in his life) in the year before his death. This quatrain also depicts Philip's parallel war against the Turks in the Mediterranean, which culminated in the success of the 1571 Battle of Lepanto. The "young onion" in 1589 (*see* index date) would have been the 36-year-old Henri IV of France (then, as now, France was renowned for its "onions"), with whom Philip was to be at bitter loggerheads until his death, eight years later.

William of Orange

DATE 1650, CENTURY I, QUATRAIN 50

"De l'aquatique triplicité naistra.
D'un qui fera le jeudi pour sa feste
Son bruit, loz, regne, sa puissance croistra,
Par terre et mer aux Oriens tempeste."

A triumvirate will arise from the water
One of whom will choose Thursday for his feast day
He will be both renowned and praised, and his reign and power
will grow The Easterners will be battered by land and by sea.

The "triumvirate/triplicity" that Nostradamus mentions may be taken both literally, in the sense of an alliance of three, and meta-phorically, in the sense of a man under the dominance of the three great environmentally and emotionally sensitive water signs of Cancer (liquid/cardinal), Scorpio (solid/fixed), and Pisces (gas/mutable). This man will choose "Thursday" for his feast day. Maundy Thursday, the day before Good Friday, is considered particularly propitious, being the day Jesus Christ commanded men and women to "love one another". In this commentator's view the quatrain refers to William III of Orange, who was born with his sun in Scorpio, on 14 November 1650, instantly succeeding his father who had died only eight days earlier of smallpox. William was later to win the English, Scottish and Irish Crowns as a result of the Glorious Revolution of 1688. The largely benevolent and religiously tolerant joint reign of William and his wife, Mary, followed by their daughter, Anne, marked the beginning of the true parliamentary period of British rule.

James I

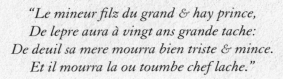

"Le mineur filz du grand & hay prince,
De lepre aura à vingt ans grande tache:
De deuil sa mere mourra bien triste & mince.
Et il mourra la ou toumbe chef lache."

The youngest son of the great and hated prince
Will be greatly marked, at twenty, by corruption
His emaciated mother will die from the sadness of her grief
And he will die where the cowardly leader falls.

The word *"leper"* in Old French meant both leprosy, and, in its figurative form, "corruption". The index date of 7 then gives us our second clue, for the youngest son of King James I of England was the future King Charles I (his younger brother having died in infancy, and his elder brother having succumbed to typhoid fever aged 18). The "great and hated prince" refers to the extreme displeasure with which King James I's suspension of Parliament, on 4 July 1607, was viewed, following its refusal to countenance union with Scotland (James, the son of Mary, Queen of Scots, had ruled Scotland as King James VI since 24 July 1567). His son Charles's mother, Anne of Denmark, died after a long period of ill health ("much wasted within, especially her liver"), in 1619, when Charles (who was very definitely her least favourite son) was rising "twenty". All in all, then, an extremely accurate quatrain depicting the complicated triangle of James I, his wife, Anne of Denmark, and their son, the future Charles I.

Frederick the Great

DATE 1757, CENTURY VIII, QUATRAIN 57

"De souldat simple parviendra en empire,
De robe courte parviendra à la longue
Vaillant aux armes en Eglise ou plus pyre,
Vexer les prestres comme l'eau fait l'esponge."

A simple soldier will attain to an empire
From short tunic he will rise to long
Brave in arms in the Church or even worse
He upset the priests as water upsets a sponge.

Adolf Hitler was a "simple soldier" during the Great War, but he does not accord with Nostradamus's index date of 57. Frederick the Great of Prussia, however, does fit the bill, as his father was so obsessed with making a "soldier" of the boy that he caused the child to be awoken every morning to the sound of cannons, and gave the six-year-old his very own regiment of children to drill. The year 1757 was a pivotal one for Frederick (despite his defeat at Kolin) with victories at Prague, Rossbach and Leuthen. The image of Frederick "upsetting the priests as water upsets a sponge" might be taken to refer to Frederick's intellectual ecumenism (he was a close friend of Voltaire) which saw him welcoming Jesuits, Huguenots, Jews, Muslims, and numerous other groups to his country. He later said that "all religions are equal and good, and so long as those practising are honest persons and wish to populate our land, be they Turks or Pagans, we will build them mosques and churches". A "sponge" indeed.

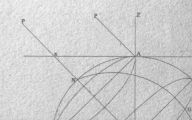

George Washington

DATE 1775, CENTURY V, QUATRAIN 75

"Montera haut sur le bien plus à dextre,
Demourra assis sur la pierre quarree:
Vers le midi posé à la fenestre,
Baston tortu en main, bouche serree."

He will rise high over the one considerably to the right of him
He will remain seated on the stone square
Towards the south, placed at the window
Crooked staff in hand, his mouth pursed.

Given the index date of 75, it is most likely that this quatrain refers to the American War of Independence, and to the election of the then left-wing George Washington as commander-in-chief of the Continental Army, over the more conservative John Hancock – an event which took placed on 15 June 1775. John Adams was taking a calculated gamble, of course, in placing Washington, a "Southerner", over an army made up largely of Northerners, but the gamble belatedly paid off when Washington successfully led the main arm

of the Continental Army across the Delaware River to destroy the Hessian conscript force at Trenton. George Washington then went on to become the first ever president of the United States. The image that Nostradamus portrays of Washington "seated on the stone square" may reasonably be taken to refer either to the famous statue, in Union Square Park, of Washington seated on his horse, dated 1865, and the oldest in the New York City Parks collection, or to the roughly similar equestrian statue in the Boston Public Garden. It would be nice to think that the "crooked staff" in line four referred to the famous Crooked Billet Inn at Hatboro, in which George Washington was known to have held a series of important staff meetings in 1777, but it is considerably more likely to refer to the crooked knobbly cane given to Washington by Benjamin Franklin, and which is held to this day in the Smithsonian Institution. Franklin described the cane as follows: "My fine crab-tree walking stick, with a gold head curiously wrought in the form of the cap of liberty, I give to my friend, and the friend of mankind, General Washington. If it were a Sceptre, he has merited it, and would become it."

Napoleon Bonaparte

"PAU, NAY, LORON plus feu qu'à sang sera.
Laude nager, fuir grand aux surrez.
Les agassas entree refusera.
Pampon, Durance les tiendra enferrez."

Pau, Nay, Loron, he will be more fire than blood
Swimming in praise, the great man hurries towards the crossroads
He will deny entry to the magpies
Pampon and Durrance will confine them.

The obvious acronym "Pau, Nay, Loron" in the first line stands for Napaulon Roy (Napoleon King – the Corsican-style spelling of Napoleon's Christian name is Napauleone, with the second part of the name referring to *leone*, a lion). The further suggestion that "he will be more fire than blood" clearly refers to Napoleon's lineage and character, which was that of a soldier ("fire"), rather than that of the nobility ("blood"). In addition to this, Napoleon was born under a "fire" sign, Leo (the lion – *see* above), which Nostradamus would have considered more than relevant. Napoleon also had Mars in Mars, or Mars in Virgo, depending on which astrological reading one adheres to, both of which go a long way towards explaining his warlike and practical nature. "*Agassa*" is the Provençal word for a magpie (or *pie*, in French), and the two *pies* are the two Piuses, both of whom were popes (Pius VI and Pius VII) whom Napoleon imprisoned and otherwise tormented during his reign, in 1798 (*see* index date) and 1809 respectively. Pius VI died barely a year after his forced deposition,

whilst Pius VII lasted somewhat longer, despite spending more than half of his time as pope bickering with Napoleon, and demanding both the release of his 13 Black Cardinals (Napoleon has deprived them of their various dignities, including their red robes), the return of the Papal States, and his own release from his exile. This is an entirely successful quatrain, therefore, cleverly dissecting Napoleon Bonaparte's ancestry, and commenting on the essential character of the one man who, more than any other, haunts the political and emotional map of France, right down to dictating the very form the French State would take in the aftermath of his death.

The Prince Regent

"Le prochain fils de l'asnier parviendra
Tant esleué jusque au regne des fors,
Son aspre gloire un chascun la craindra,
Mais ses enfants du regne getés hors."

The next son will succeed his elder
Exceptionally, he will be raised to reign
His rough glory will make all fear his effect
His children will be thrown out.

In 1810 King George III of England fell ill once again, suffering from hallucinations caused by the hereditary disease of porphyria. The attack was so severe that in early 1811 Parliament decided on a new Regency Act designed to make George's son, George Augustus Frederick, prince regent for the second time. Profligate and wilful, the Prince Regent had secretly married the twice-widowed Roman Catholic Mrs Fitzherbert, in 1785, but the marriage had long been considered void in the absence of his father's royal consent. In ever-increasing debt, the Prince Regent was forced to accept his father's stipulation that he marry his cousin, Caroline of Brunswick. The marriage proved disastrous, and the warring parties were legally separated after the birth of their only child, Princess Charlotte. The Prince Regent sired a number of illegitimate children, but these were "thrown out" to make way for George's brother, William, who was not allowed to hand on the throne to any of *his* nine illegitimate children either. The crown eventually passed to his niece, Princess Victoria.

Hitler's Agenda

DATE 1920, CENTURY II, QUATRAIN 20

"Freres et soeurs en divers lieux captifs
Se trouveront passer pres du monarque:
Les contempler ses rameaux ententifs,
Desplaisant voir menton, front, nez, les marques."

Brothers and sisters held captive in various places
They pass near the monarch
He looks at them with alert attention
It is disagreeable to see the marks on forehead, nose, and face.

When Nostradamus speaks of "marks" it is likely that he is referring to the "mark of the beast", i.e. 666, as defined in Revelations xiii: 18. Many consider the number to be an example of Hebrew *gematria* (numerology), which was often used to disguise the "revealed" rather than the "mystical" (i.e. the kabbalistic) form of a given name. Nostradamus considered Adolf Hitler to be the Second Antichrist, so we must look to 1920 (given the index date) for an explanation of this quatrain. And in February 1920 we find that Hitler presented his National Socialist agenda for the first time in Munich. This agenda was heavily based on the writings of Martin Luther (particularly on his treatise entitled *On The Jews And Their Lies* 1543), in which Luther proclaimed the following: "The reason why I did not then perceive the absurdity of such an illusion [i.e. of considering Jews as ordinary human beings] was that the only external mark which I recognized as distinguishing them from us was the practice of their strange religion."

Lenin Dies

DATE 1924, CENTURY V, QUATRAIN 24

"Le regne & loys soubz Venus esleué,
Saturne aura sur Iupiter empire:
La loy & regne par le Soleil leué,
Par Saturnins endurera le pire."

Both reign and law are raised up under Venus
Saturn will hold the ascendancy over Jupiter
Both law and reign raised by the sun
The Saturnians will cause no end of trouble.

We are back with evil "Saturn" again, a theme to which Nostradamus returns on numerous occasions during the course of his quatrains. In fact one is reminded of these lines from Book IV of Alexander Pope's *The Dunciad*: *Then rose the Seed of Chaos and of Night / To blot out order and extinguish light, / Of dull and venal a new world to mould, / And bring Saturnian days of lead and gold.* Saturn, you may recall, ate his own children, save only for "Jupiter", Neptune, and Pluto – Jupiter, in this context, stands in for "air", and time (ergo Saturn/Kronos) cannot consume him, of course, because of his stark invisibility. Pope is referring in line four of his poem to Saturn's Tree, which is the alchemical massing of crystallized "lead", a substance which was considered to give rise to "dullness", with gold (ergo the "sun"), suggesting "venality". With all this as ammunition, and an index date of 24, one finds oneself seamlessly carried to 1924, and the Russian Revolution – a case of Saturnian ascendancy, if ever there was one – and to the death, on 21 January, of Chairman of the Council of

People's Commissars, Vladimir Ilyich Lenin. Nostradamus's cannibalistic image then comes rightly into its own, with Saturn's (ergo Lenin's) notional children, Jupiter, Neptune and Pluto – in the form of Joseph Stalin, Grigori Zinoviev, and Leon Trotsky – all vying for power in Lenin's stead. This is a wonderful quatrain, therefore, both metaphorically and index date accurate, about the battle for power in Soviet Russia following the death, in 1924, of Vladimir Ilyich Lenin, following a series of strokes undoubtedly triggered by two bullet wounds he had received (one of a number of failed assassination attempts) six years earlier, on 30 August 1918.

The Third Reich

"Hercules Roy de Rome & d'Annemarc,
De Gaule trois Guion surnommé,
Trembler l'Italie & l'unde de sainct Marc,
Premier sur tous monarque renommé."

King Hercules of Rome and Mark Anthony
Three leaders of France are surnamed Guyon
Italy and the location of Saint Marc will tremble
First amongst all is the monarch's renown.

There never was a "Hercules" who was king of "Rome" and of Denmark, so we are talking of a "Herculean" figure here, and not an eponymous king. The "Denmark/*d'Annemarc*" clue also seems a false one, as we know that Mark Antony ("*annemarc*" reversed) became obsessed by Hercules, and even gave Hercules a fictional son, Anton, from whom Cleopatra's lover claimed distant ancestry. "*Guyon*" means a guide or a leader in Old French, and "*unde*" comes from the Latin, and means "from whence", which, in the context of "St Mark's", usually means Venice. So we are speaking of a series of strong leaders who share an index date of 33. Albrecht von Wallenstein in 1633? Augustus the Strong of Poland, who died in 1733? Or is this more sinister, relating to the declaration, by Adolf Hitler, of the Third Reich, on 15 March 1933 (remember that Hitler was known as *der Führer*, meaning a guide or leader). Hitler/der Führer/Guyon did indeed become the titular leader of France, and he certainly made Italy, Venice, and Rome tremble.

General Franco

DATE 1936, CENTURY IX, QUATRAIN 16

"De castel Franco sortira l'assemblee
L'ambassadeur non plaisant fera scisme
Ceux de Ribiere seront en la meslee
Et au grand goulphre desnier ont l'entrée."

Franco will force the assembly out of Castile
The outraged ambassador will create a schism
Rivera's men will form part of the free-for-all
The leader will be refused entry to the gulf.

This is one of the most famous of all Nostradamus's quatrains, for it mentions both Francisco "Franco" (1892–1975), self-proclaimed *Caudillo de España, por la gracia de Dios*, and Primo de "Rivera" (1870–1930), Franco's marginally less dictatorial predecessor. When Rivera died, his son, José Antonio, recreated the Falange movement in his father's honour, fighting alongside Franco during the Spanish Civil War of 1936–39. Franco became dictator of all of Spain in 1939 following the halt of hostilities, remaining in control for a further 36 years. The "outraged ambassador" in line two undoubtedly refers to the series of foreign interventions that were to mark the Spanish Civil War, and that included the German carpet-bombing of Guernica. The last line refers to the 1936 Spanish Republican Government's exile of Franco to the Canary Islands, thus denying him entry to the Mediterranean "gulf". The Spanish would later look on Rivera's benevolent autocracy with nostalgic fondness, given the unremittingly severe dictatorship that ensued.

Abdication Crisis

DATE 1936, CENTURY II, QUATRAIN 36

"Du grand Prophete les letres seront prinses
Entre les mains du tyran deviendront:
Frauder son roy seront ses entreprinses,
Mais ses rapines bien tost le troubleront."

The letters are taken by the great Prophet
They will come into the hands of the tyrant
He will endeavour to defraud his king
But his robberies will soon cause him trouble.

The index date of 36 takes us to 3 December 1936, and to the breaking of silence by the British press ("the great Prophet") on the subject of King Edward VIII's infatuation with Mrs Wallis Simpson, his intended future wife. On 13 November, the king's private secretary, Alec Hardinge, had written to the king warning him that: "The silence in the British Press on the subject of Your Majesty's friendship with Mrs Simpson is not going to be maintained ... Judging by the letters from British subjects living in foreign countries where the Press has been outspoken, the effect will be calamitous." This culminated in the famous "letter" of abdication that Edward wrote, and which was signed by the king and his three brothers. The "tyrant" is Stanley Baldwin, who made it clear to the king that he could not marry a twice-divorced woman and hope to continue on as King of England. The king broadcast his decision to abdicate on 11 December, and Baldwin retired from his Prime Ministership less than five months later.

Erwin Rommel

DATE 1941, CENTURY VIII, QUATRAIN 41

"Esleu sera Renad, ne sonnant mot,
Faisant le saint public vivant pain d'orge,
Tyrannizer apres tant à un cop,
Mettant à pied des plus grans sus la gorge."

The fox will be elected, without saying a word
Made into a saint by the public, he lives on barley bread
He will be tyrannized some time later after a coup
The great ones trampling on his throat.

A splendid quatrain, in which the index date of 41 and the codeword "fox" take us directly to the year 1941, and to the victories of Erwin Rommel, nicknamed the Desert "Fox". By 15 April that year Rommel had secured the whole of Libya, a success that resulted in his "election", in August, to the role of Commander Panzer Group Afrika. Curiously, the word "fox" was to reappear again in Rommel's life when his car was strafed, and Rommel seriously injured, by an RCAF Spitfire piloted by Charley Fox (Charley is the rural nickname for a fox in England, so the pilot was in fact "Foxy Fox"!). Nostradamus then describes the upshot of the "coup" against Adolf Hitler which was to cost Rommel his life ("some time later"), when his superiors forced him to commit suicide ("the great ones trampling on his throat") after he may – or may not – have been involved in the 20 July assassination plot against the Führer. There followed a hero's burial, with Hitler playing a major part in the proceedings.

Adolf Hitler

DATE 1945, CENTURY II, QUATRAIN 24

"Bestes farouches de faim fluves tranner:
Plus part du camp encontre Hister sera,
En caige de fer le grand sera treisner,
Quand Rin enfant Germain observera."

With the hunger of wild beasts they will cross the rivers
Most of the country will be against Hister
The great man will find himself paraded inside a cage of iron
The German child [of the Rhine] will see nothing.

A justifiably famous quatrain which twins the four "rivers" of the Rhine, the Danube, the Elbe, and the Vistula, with those who both cross, and are of them. The quatrain brings together Adolf Hitler, Benito Mussolini, and Germany's eventual nemesis, the embittered and brutalized Russian army, in a clear depiction of the final catastrophic year of the Second World War. The quatrain links the word "Hister" (Hitler/Danube) with "German", and it also describes the fate of Adolf Hitler's chief ally, Benito Mussolini, whose manner of death is accurately described as being "paraded inside a cage of iron" (following the shooting of Mussolini and his mistress, Clara Petacci, in Guilino di Mezzegra, near Lake Como, Italy, just two days before Hitler's own death, their bodies were taken back to Milan and hung on meat hooks in the charred metal frame of a fire-bombed petrol station in the Piazzale Loreto). "*Hister*" has a further link to Hitler, however, beyond the euphonic, for it was the Latin name for the Danube River – Hitler was born on a tributary of the Danube (Braunau Am Inn)

and grew up on its banks, in Linz. Line one takes the river symbolism even further, for it clearly refers to the Russian army, which crossed the Elbe and the Vistula rivers in 1945 ("they will cross the rivers") as part of their push into Germany, before raping "like wild beasts" many tens of thousands of German women in a coldly premeditated revenge for the horrors of Stalingrad. The last line is a particularly haunting one, as it appears to echo the reiterated statement made by millions of Germans after the war that they had no actual knowledge of Hitler's so-called Final Solution ("the German child sees nothing").

End of the Third Reich

DATE 1945, CENTURY V, QUATRAIN 45

"Le grand Empire sera tost désolé,
Et translaté pres d'arduer ne silve
Les deux bastardz par l'aisné decollé,
Et regnera Aenobarbe, nay de milve."

The great Empire will be completely devastated
And transformed near the Ardennes into disparate pieces
The two spurious ones will be beheaded by their senior
Aenobarbus, the kite-born [hawk-nosed] one, will reign.

The Latin word for the Ardennes Forest was *"Ardvenna Silva"*, which is the likely meaning of what may well be a typographical error (it was rectified in later editions of *The Centuries*). However *ardu* is also an Old French adjective meaning arduous, *ne* means not, and *silves*, as well as meaning the same as *silva*, a wood, can also means a collection of disparate pieces – and we know how Nostradamus likes his puns and his wordplays! With all that said, this quatrain is clearly about the destruction of the Third Reich in 1945 ("the great Empire will be completely devastated"), following the failure of von Rundstedt's deadly "Ardennes" campaign of 16 December 1944 to 25 January 1945. The "two spurious ones" are Hitler and Mussolini, both of whom were to die within two days of each other, and barely three months after the events mentioned here. Aenobarbus means "the bronze-bearded one", and one wonders whether the "kite-born/hawk-nosed" man who will reign after the destruction of Germany in 1945 is not Stalin – the "steel man".

Nicolas Sarkozy

DATE 2014, CENTURY III, QUATRAIN 14

"Par le rameau du vaillant personnage
De France infime; par le pere infelice:
Honneurs, richesses, travail en son vieil aage
Pour avoir creu le conseil d'homme nice."

Via the branch of the valiant person
From the lowest part of France; through an unhappy father
Honours, riches, he will work into old age
Thanks to his faith in the counsel of the foolish man.

Nicolas Sarkozy was elected 23rd French President on 16 May 2007, meaning that he will be up for re-election again in 2012. By 2014 he will be 59 years old, and as there is no term limit for French presidents, he might conceivably still be in office as late as 2022 ("he will work into old age"), aged 77. Sarkozy's background includes Hungarian, Greek, and Jewish ancestry. His "unhappy father", Pál Sárközy, an aristocratic ex-Foreign Legionnaire, abandoned his wife and family in 1959, and Sarkozy saw little of him thereafter. The "foolish man", whose influence nevertheless ensured Sarkozy's success, might therefore be the Alpes-Maritimes-born Charles Pasqua (*l'homme nice* – Pasqua was born in Grasse, 20 kilometres as the crow flies behind Nice, "the lowest part of France"), whose inconvenient illness – twinned with a desire to have Sarkozy run his mayoral campaign – allowed Sarkozy to pip him to the post as mayor of Neuilly-Sur-Seine in 1983, a position Sarkozy held until 2002, and which was to prove his launching pad to higher office.

MURDERS, MASSACRES and MACHINATIONS

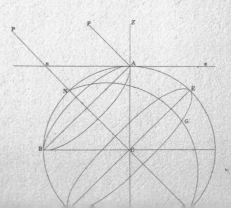

Suleiman the Magnificent

DATE 1559, CENTURY III, QUATRAIN 59

"Barbare empire par le tiers usurpé,
La plus grand part de son sang metra à mort:
Par mort senile par luy le quart frappé,
Pour peur que sang par le sang ne soit mort."

The third one usurps the Barbarian empire
He will put most of his relations to death
Then the old man strikes dead the fourth
For fear that the line hasn't been killed off by one of its own.

This is about Suleiman the Magnificent, and the murder of his firstborn son, Mustafa, in order that the sons of his favourite concubine and later wife, Hurrem Sultan (a.k.a. Roxelana), could inherit the Ottoman Empire. Mustafa was the son of Suleiman's first wife, Gülbahar Sultan, and therefore the legal heir. He was a man of such distinction that the Austrian ambassador, wrote: "May God never allow a Barbary [*see* line one] of such strength to come near us." Following Mustafa's death by strangulation (which Suleiman ordered and watched), one half-brother, Jihangir, died of grief a few months later, whilst the other two half-brothers, Selim and Bayezid, began to fight amongst themselves. In 1559 Selim finally defeated Bayezid, who, along with his four sons, took refuge with the Persians. Suleiman then paid the Shah of Persia a vast sum to have all five of them put to death, leaving the way clear for Selim to succeed him, seven years later.

Henri II of France

DATE 1559, CENTURY I, QUATRAIN 35

"Le lion jeune le vieux surmontera,
En champ bellique par singulier duelle:
Dans caige d'or les yeux lui crevera,
Deux classes une, puis mourir, mort cruelle."

The young lion will overcome the old one
Hand to hand, on the field of combat
His eyes will burst in their golden helmet
Two breaks in one, followed by a merciless death.

Published a full three years before the fateful death it foretold, this is the famous quatrain detailing the death, in a joust, of King Henri II of France. Despite repeated warnings from both Nostradamus, his queen, and his Italian court astrologer, Luca Gaurico, the virile 41-year-old king insisted on taking an active part in the three-day tournament celebrating the double marriages of his sister and eldest daughter. Galvanized by his success in the first two days of the jousting, Henri challenged Gabriel de Lorge, Count of Montgomery, and captain of his Scottish Guard, to ritual single combat on the third and final day of the tournament. At the very last moment, sensing disaster, the 35-year-old Montgomery tried to avoid the king's person, but his lance caught on the lip of Henri's helmet, splintering on his visor, and entering the king's right orbit and temple, just above the right eye. Despite prompt treatment by Master Surgeon Ambroise Paré, and Philip II's great anatomist, Andreas Vesalius, Henri died an agonizing death on 10 July 1559.

Witch Trials at Aix

DATE 1611, CENTURY II, QUATRAIN 10

"Avant long temps le tout sera rangé,
Nous esperons un siecle bien senestre:
L'estat des masques & des seulz bien changé
Peu trouveront qu'a son rang veuille estre."

Everything will be sorted out before too long
We can expect a bastard century
The status of witches and of priests will change
Not many will wish to remain at their given station.

The Old French word *"masque"* has, as one of its many origins, the Old Provençal word *masco*, meaning a witch – a word with which the Provençal-born Nostradamus would have been achingly familiar as a result of the numerous witch trials that plagued the area around his birthplace during the 15th and 16th centuries. The index date, and the linking of the words "witches" and "priests", takes us straight to the trial of Father Louis Gaufridi at Aix-en-Provence, for allegedly sending devils to possess the local Ursuline nuns. After surviving torture by varying forms of strappado, Gaufridi was towed around the city for five hours before being burnt at the stake on 30 April 1611. Nostradamus is right on the money in suggesting that the 17th century will be a "bastard" one, for the years 1600 to 1625 represented the peak of the French witch-hunting pogroms which, like those at Loudon, concentrated on priests and nuns in particular (a connection we are afforded via the Old French expression *"les seuls"*, meaning those who live a celibate life).

Plague Infectors

DATE 1614, CENTURY IX, QUATRAIN 14

"Mys en planure chaulderons d'infecteurs,
Vin, miel & huyle, & bastis sur forneaulx
Seront plongez sans mal dit mal facteurs
Sept. fum extaint au canon des borneaux."

The infectors are placed in cauldrons, upon shavings
Wine, honey and oil, built on furnaces
The malefactors will be plunged in with no further ado
Seven extinguished by smoke from the executioner's tube.

In the 16th century the eminent Catholic Bernard de la Roche Flavin, a long-term member of the *parlement* of Toulouse, wrote that those accused of passing on plague infections ("the infectors") were routinely burnt alive over a slow flame (*Letters – Book III*). He counselled moderation, however, claiming that any form of torture was "a dangerous invention", even in the case of a *crimen exceptum* such as plague promulgation. We certainly know that both Toulouse and Claremont suffered a plague outbreak between 1610 and 1620, as Irish physician Nial O'Glacan says so in his famous *Tractatus de Peste*. O'Glacan was later appointed to the Toulouse Chair of Medicine, before becoming Physician in Ordinary to the King, and it seems clear, in retrospect, that Nostradamus is describing something resembling the plague potions O'Glacan details in his book, twinned with the tortures so condemned by de la Roche Flavin. A wonderful quatrain, therefore, showing just how seriously plague promulgation was viewed in southwestern France during the 16th and 17th centuries.

Defenestration of Prague

DATE 1618, CENTURY VII, QUATRAIN 18

"Les assiegés couloureront leur paches,
Sept iours apres feront cruelle issue:
Dans repousé, feu sang, sept mis à l'ache,
Dame captive qu'avoit la paix tissue."

The besieged ones will disguise their pacts
Seven day afterwards they will make a cruel sortie
In the return push, fire, blood, seven put to the axe
The lady who laced the peace together is captured.

The word *"ache"* in line three means both "put to the axe" and "hanged", as in Old French the term *Achéen* meant Achean, and related to Acheus, King of Lydia, who was hanged by his subjects for extortion. The "cruel sortie" in line two is a sublime pun on the 23 May 1618 Defenestration of Prague, which saw the Holy Roman Emperor's two regents in Prague, Jaroslav Martinic and Vilém Slawata, together with their scribe, Philip Fabricius, thrown out of the high windows of the Council Room of Hradcany Castle. The three men landed in a manure heap and survived, with Fabricius later being ennobled by the emperor under the ironical name of von Hohenfall (von Highfall). Interestingly, there had been a previous Defenestration of Prague in 1419, which saw the killing of "seven" members of the city council, and which had been triggered by a procession led by a Hussite priest from the Church of the Virgin Mary of the Snows ("the captured lady"). Nostradamus links together both events here, and highlights the obvious parallels.

Charles I's Future

DATE 1637, CENTURY VIII, QUATRAIN 37

"La forteresse aupres de la Tamise
Cherra par lors le Roy dedans serré,
Aupres du pont sera veu en chemise
Un devant mort, puis dans le fort barré."

The fortress near the Thames
Will be cherished when the king is held within it
He will be seen in his shirt near the bridge
One earlier death, then in the stronghold turned into a prison.

The "fortress near the Thames" sounds very much like the Tower of London, and the "stronghold turned into a prison" like the Palace of Whitehall. This is Nostradamus thinking himself forward to the year 1637, and then looking ahead again at what will happen in the 12 years after that. We now know that the ensuing years were crucial pointers in terms of Charles I's eventual fate, and that the "one earlier death" at the Tower is that of Thomas Wentworth, Earl of Strafford, who was beheaded in 1641 (a precedent indeed). When Charles met his own executioner on 30 January 1649 ("in his shirt", which was later exhibited on a pole on London "Bridge"), he opined that God had permitted his own execution as just punishment for signing the loyal Strafford's death warrant. This is a particularly prescient quatrain, therefore, which describes two key buildings (the Tower of London and the Palace of Whitehall) that were to figure in King Charles I's life and death over the course of the next 12 years.

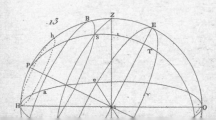

Charles I's Execution

DATE 1649, CENTURY IX, QUATRAIN 49

"Gand & Bruceles marcheront contre Envers
Senat de Londres meteront à mort leur roy,
Le sel & vin luy seront à l'envers,
Pour eux avoir le regne en desarroy."

Ghent and Brussels march against the wrong side
The London parliament will put their king to death
Salt and wine will become mixed up
They will take over the realm in the confusion.

By any view – jaundiced, retroactive, or just plain malicious – this quatrain must surely convince even dyed-in-the-wool sceptics of Nostradamus's extraordinary powers of prescience. His index date is 49. His second line reads "The London Parliament will put their king to death". And Charles I of England was indeed put to death on 30 January 1649 by order of the London Parliament. When was the quatrain published? In 1568, in Lyon, by Benoist Rigaud, two years after Nostradamus's death, and a full 81 years before the event described. That is categorical enough for anyone, surely? Line one refers to the final stages of the Thirty Years' War, which culminated with the Battle of Lens ("Ghent", "Brussels" and Lens form a perfect triangle in French Flanders). The reference to "salt" and "wine" being mixed up is a reference to "sitting above the salt", meaning to sit in a place of distinction (ergo the throne – it must be remembered that Charles was an advocate of the divine right of kings, and was canonized by the Church of England in 1660, becoming St Charles

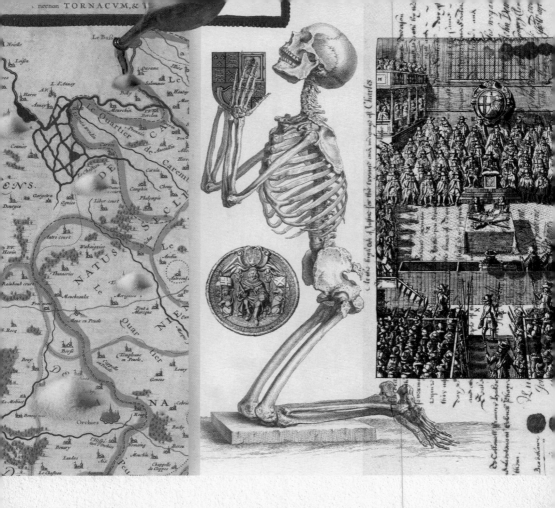

Stuart), and also to the Roman habit of mixing wine with myrrh (*vinum myrrha conditum*), which was then given to those about to be executed or crucified in order to deaden their sufferings (*see* Mark xv. 23). Charles's last words add further emphasis to his belief that his martyrdom echoed that of Christ: "I shall go from a corruptible to an incorruptible Crown, where no disturbance can be." One of the greatest of all Nostradamus's quatrains, therefore, predicting the exact date of the death of King Charles I of England, and also of the "taking over of the realm" by the Commonwealth of England on the very same day.

Charles XII of Sweden

DATE 1718, CENTURY V, QUATRAIN 18

"De dueil mourra l'infelix profligé,
Celebrera son vitrix l'heccatombe:
Pristine loy franc edict redigé,
Le mur & Prince au septiesme iour tombe."

The unhappily overthrown one dies grieving
The victorious woman celebrates the sacrifice
The primitive Frankish law is formally drawn up
Both the Prince and the wall fall on the seventh day.

An extraordinary quatrain, index-date perfect, depicting the death, during the 1718 siege of the Norwegian fortress of Frederiksten, of Swedish King Charles XII. Charles was apparently struck by a musket ball while inspecting trenches close to the "walls" of the fortress, however there is some speculation that he was killed by one of his own side, and not by a Norwegian marksman. Either way, his sister, Ulrike Leonore ("the victrix"), was the main beneficiary of his death (as was her husband, the soon-to-be Frederick I, who may have had a hand in Charles's death, if assassination it was), as she succeeded to the Swedish throne in his stead. The Palatinate-Zweibrücken, over which her brother had also ruled, required a male heir, however, thanks to the "primitive Frankish law" of male-preference primogeniture, and Charles's cousin, Gustav Leopold, duly took over in his stead. A stunningly accurate quatrain which shows how Ulrike Leonore, sister of King Charles XII of Sweden, benefited by his untimely death during the siege of the fortress of Frederiksten.

Assassination of Lincoln

DATE 1865, CENTURY IV, QUATRAIN 65

"Au deserteur de la grand fortresse,
Apres qu'aura son lieu abandonné:
Son adversaire fera si gran prouesse,
L'Empereur tost mort sera condemné."

To the one who deserted the great fortress
After he left his post
His opponent will make such a show of prowess
That the doomed Emperor will be condemned.

The "doomed Emperor" is Abraham Lincoln (Nostradamus would not have understood the concept of a president), and the act that, with the benefit of historical hindsight, "will condemn" him, was the surrender of the Confederate forces under General Robert E. Lee at Appomattox courthouse, on 9 April 1865 (*see* index date). A mere five days later, on 14 April (Good Friday), President Lincoln was assassinated at Ford's Theatre, in Washington DC, by the embittered actor and Confederate spy, John Wilkes Booth, at a predetermined laugh-out-loud moment in the performance of Tom Taylor's comedy, *Our American Cousin*. Booth, who had broken his leg whilst leaping from the Lincolns's box in an effort to evade capture – at the same moment he had famously shouted *sic semper tyrannis* ("thus do tyrants always reap their just deserts") – paid for the act with his life, 12 days later, whilst "resisting" arrest. Lincoln was the first US President to be assassinated, and the first to lie in state – a privilege which, until then, had been granted only to "Emperors" and kings.

Night of the Long Knives

DATE 1934, CENTURY VIII, QUATRAIN 34

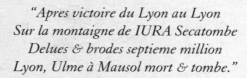

"Apres victoire du Lyon au Lyon
Sur la montaigne de IURA Secatombe
Delues & brodes septieme million
Lyon, Ulme à Mausol mort & tombe."

After the victory of the lion over the lion
There will be oath-taking in the mountain hecatomb
The deluge and embroidery of the seventh million
Lion, Ulm to the Mausoleum, death and tomb.

The two "lions" are Adolf Hitler and Ernst Röhm, and Hitler chose the night of 30 June 1934 to bring Röhm, and his out-of-control Storm Detachment, the SA, to heel, via Operation Hummingbird. Eighty-five died in the purge (SA-hecatomb, ergo *"Secatombe"*) with thousands more arrested. Röhm, after refusing to take his own life, was executed at Stadelheim prison two days later. The "oath-taking on the mountain" is that of the now resurgent SS at Schloss Wewelsburg, their spiritual home, and the mention of the "seventh million" in line three, alongside the "deluge", and the "embroidery" (Jewish bodies are covered with a hand-sewn cloth similar to that worn by the high priest in the temple at Yom Kippur), represents the approximate number of Jews killed during the whole of World War Two as part of Hitler's so-called Final Solution. An extraordinary quatrain, clearly anticipating the future horrors of World War Two – horrors which became inevitable following Hitler's consolidation of power during what was to become known as the Night of the Long Knives.

de Gaulle's Close Shave

DATE 1962, CENTURY IV, QUATRAIN 62

"Un coronel machine ambition,
Se saisira de la plus grand armée:
Contre son prince fainte invention,
Et descouvert sera soubz la ramée."

An ambitious and intriguing colonel
Will get hold of the grand army
He will falsely contrive against his prince
And will end up beneath the trees.

This quatrain reeks of the assassination attempt on President Charles de Gaulle, on 22 August 1962 (*see* index date). The attempt was triggered after de Gaulle, in September 1959, backtracked on his undertaking to maintain Algeria as "an integral part of France", angering both *Pieds-Noirs* (white Algerian colonists feeling doubly alienated from both France *and* Algeria) and elements of the French Army, which was still smarting from its 1954 defeat at Dien Bien Phu, in French Indochina. The OAS (*L'Organisation de l'Armée Secrète*) was responsible, and one of the putative assassins, Jean-Marie Bastien-Thiry (a member of the ultra-secret *Vieil État-Major*), with other leaders of the OAS, were subsequently executed by firing squad. Amongst the officers commanding the OAS (Metropolitan French, Algerian, and Spanish branches), were seven "colonels", of whom Colonels Godard and Gardes were the highest-placed. The failed assassination was later depicted in Frederick Forsyth's 1971 novel, *The Day of the Jackal*, and the eponymous 1973 movie.

The Montagnards

DATE 1963, CENTURY IV, QUATRAIN 63

"L'armée Celtique contre les montaignars,
Qui seront sceuz & prins à la lipee
Paysans fresz pousseront tost faugnars,
Precipitez tous au fil de l'espee."

The Celtic army against the Montagnards
Who will be sealed in and taken by a trick
Fresh peasants will soon push back the press
All will be swept onto the point of a sword.

The word "Montagnards" takes us to the central highlands of Vietnam, as does the index date of 63. For it was in 1963 that the US Special Forces (part of the "Celtic army", with *Celtique* used in the sense of "foreign"), first decided to use the Degar (Vietnam's indigenous mountain tribespeople) against the Vietcong. To accomplish this, certain elements of the Green Berets, under orders from the CIA, poisoned 40 Montagnard schoolchildren and their teachers and blamed it on the Vietcong (*see* my article in the *Sunday Times Magazine* of 13 February 2000, entitled "An American Hero"). The Montagnard tribesmen took a terrible revenge on every member of the Vietcong they ran into after that period, and were duly rewarded for their support of US Forces by being abandoned at the end of the war, in 1975, with thousands forced to flee across the border to Cambodia or risk being resettled or massacred. A brilliant quatrain, then, depicting the link between US Special Forces and Vietnamese Montagnards during the early stages of the Vietnam war.

Assassination of JFK

DATE 1963, CENTURY VI, QUATRAIN 37

"L'oeuvre ancienne se parachevera,
Du toict cherra sur le grand mal ruyne:
Innocent faict mort on accusera:
Nocent caiché, taillis à la bruyne."

The ancient task will be completed
From on high, evil will fall on the great man
A dead innocent will be accused of the deed
The guilty one will remain hidden in the mist.

The killing shot, during the assassination of President John F. Kennedy, which took place in Dallas, Texas, at 12.30 pm CST, on 22 November 1963, undoubtedly came from roof level ("from on high"), entering the President's head from the rear and exiting through his brain ("evil will fall on the great man"). However the man accused of the crime, Lee Harvey Oswald, did not live long enough to testify or to proclaim his innocence in court, for he was killed in police custody by Dallas nightclub owner Jack Ruby. Before his death, Oswald persistently claimed that he was a patsy (Nostradamus's "dead innocent"), and had been set up to take the fall. Many commentators subsequently felt that the contract on the President had been ordered by the Mafia, who were angry at losing their stronghold in Cuba, and also at Bobby Kennedy's crackdown on organized crime. If this is the case, then Nostradamus's "ancient task" takes on a new dimension, as it is traditionally the head of the family who is targeted in Mafia hits.

REVOLUTION, RIOTS and RAPINE

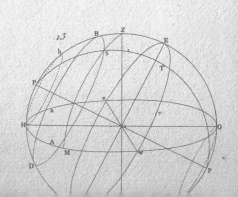

A Failed Kidnap

DATE 1560, CENTURY VI, QUATRAIN 60

"Le Prins hors de son terroir Celtique,
Sera trahy deceu par interprete:
Rouan, Rochelle par ceulx de l'Armorique,
Au port de Blaue deceuz par moine & prebstre."

The Prince, outside his Celtic homeland
Will be let down and betrayed by his interpreter
Rouen, La Rochelle, by those of Brittany
The port of La Baule will be deceived by monk and priest.

This quatrain reflects on the religious upheavals that rocked France in 1560, following the death, in a joust, of King Henri II. This culminated in a failed Huguenot conspiracy to save his son, the briefly-regnant Francis II, now aged sixteen, from the clutches of the Catholic de Guise family. Francis was a sickly young man, and easily manipulable, and the Huguenots felt that if they got hold of him, they might, just might, be able to secure some valuable concessions from the Catholic ascendancy. Francis II's "Celtic homeland" was Scotland, of which he was legally king-consort, thanks to his marriage to Mary Stuart, Queen of Scots. The marriage was fruitless, however, and it was later alleged that Francis's testicles may not have descended in proper order. The Port of "La Baule" is at the mouth of the Loire, down which the Huguenots intended to ship Francis from his alleged "incarceration" at Amboise. Francis developed an ear infection, however, which soon moved to his brain, and which resulted in his death on 5 December, at Orléans.

Huguenot Massacre

DATE 1572, CENTURY I, QUATRAIN 72

"Du tout Marseille des habitants changée,
Course & poursuitte iusques au pres de Lyon.
Narbo, Tholoze par Bourdeaux outragee:
Tués captifz presque d'un milion."

The inhabitants of all Marseille change
Flight and pursuit to near Lyon
Narbonne, Bordeaux outrages Toulouse
Nearly a million captives are killed.

This brilliant, index-date-perfect quatrain, relates directly to the 23–25 August 1572 Massacre of the Huguenots. Firstly, it ought to be pointed out that to a medieval Frenchman, just as to world traveller Marco Polo, the number of a "million" would have meant an indeterminate, but significant, number. The reality, however, was still considerable, especially if one counts the knock-on effects of the hundreds of subsidiary Protestant massacres throughout provincial France. Major massacres occurred in "Toulouse", "Bordeaux", "Lyon", Bourges, Rouen, and Orléans, with minor massacres at "Marseille" and "Narbonne". The tally varies wildly, according to source, but probably involved between 10,000 and 100,000 people. These further massacres, which took place over a considerable period, appeared to depend as much on distance from Paris for their inception as on any specifically anti-Huguenot rancour, and were equally concerned with land-grabbing, grudge-repaying, and a general outpouring of hatred against those who chose to live differently from the norm.

Charles IX/Francis I

DATE 1572, CENTURY X, QUATRAIN 72

"L'an mil neuf cens nonante neuf sept mois,
Du ciel viendra un grand Roy deffraieur
Resusciter le grand Roy d'Angolmois.
Avant après, Mars regner par bon heur."

In the seventh month of 1999
A great king of terror will descend from the sky
Reanimating the great king of Angoulème
Before and after, Mars will reign for a good hour.

This is one of the most famous of all Nostradamus's quatrains because it appears to mention an exact date. Its serial mistranslation led to a certain amount of panic in July 1999, when various simple souls managed to convince themselves that it depicted the end of the world. It depicts no such thing. Armageddon is indeed concealed within the quatrain, but numerologically, in the sense of "the one" (1) and the mirror reversal of 999, giving us 666 (ergo the devil's number) – it's a Christadelphian concept, amongst many others, and implies that there is no devil beyond the one that looks back at us when we look into the mirror. "Seven", too, is a significant holy number, and much used by Nostradamus, and the "great king of Angoulème" is merely renaissance humanist King Francis I of France (note the "1" again), whose grandson, Charles IX, allowed his mother, Catherine de Medici, alongside Henry, Duke of Guise, to unleash merry hell on the Huguenots during the Saint Bartholomew's Day Massacre of 23 to 25 August 1572.

Toulouse Massacre

"Encor seront les saincts temples pollus,
Et expillez par Senat Tholossain,
Saturne deux trois cicles revollus,
Dans Avril, May, gens de nouveau levain."

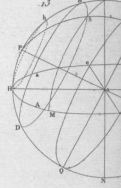

Once more the holy temples are polluted
And plundered out by the Toulouse senate
Saturn makes two or three cycles
In April, May, people of the new yeast.

The index date here coincides exactly with the Massacre of the Huguenots, which took place between 23 and 25 August 1572, in Paris, and which then spread like wildfire throughout the provinces of France, with subsidiary massacres taking place in Toulouse, Bordeaux, Lyon, Orleans, Rouen, and Bourges. The first president of the Toulouse *parlement* tried to oppose the slaughter in his city, but was overruled by the senate, and the massacre occurred on 23 September. The Huguenot connection is further strengthened by Nostradamus's use of the word "temple" for church (a traditionally Protestant usage). This is the story of the Toulouse massacres, then, which took place a month after the first Massacre of the Huguenots in Paris – massacres that were not done in hot blood, but in cold blood, after preliminary detentions at the Conciergerie. Contemporary sources put the numbers butchered by axe, cutlass, and noose at around 300. Nostradamus's use of the term "people of the new yeast" is a nice conceit for a people – the Huguenots – rising against the "older" tide of Catholicism.

Uluç Ali Reis

"Selin monarque l'Italie pacifique,
Regnes unis Roy chrestien du monde:
Mourrant vouldra coucher en terre blesique,
Apres pirates avoir chassé de l'onde."

The Selin king from a peaceful Italy
Christian kingdoms of the world are united
He will wish to die lying in a cornfield
After the pirates have been chased from the sea.

Most of medieval Christian Europe had found itself harassed, at one time or another, by the Barbary pirates ("Christian kingdoms of the world are united"). What most frustrated the Christian powers was that many of the "pirates" were forcibly converted northerners who had expediently changed allegiance for a share of the plunder the corsairs were so explicitly enjoying. This fact stuck in the European craw. So Nostradamus is engaging in something like wishful thinking in this quatrain ("after the pirates have been chased from the sea"), which is still sufficiently close in index date to the catastrophic Ottoman defeat at the Battle of Lepanto in 1571 to benefit from the psychological knock-on effects. One of the most famous Ottoman corsairs was Uluç (Euldj) Ali Reis (Reis means Admiral). He was very active in the years 1576–78 (despite Lepanto, from which he emerged with credit), and the ex-Barbary hostage Miguel de Cervantes Saavedra mentions him in his masterpiece, *Don Quixote*. Uluç Ali is Nostradamus's "Selin king from a peaceful Italy" (Selin means "crescent moon", the symbol

of the Ottoman Empire), having been born in Calabria as Giovanni Dionigi Galeni, before being captured, aged 17, and forcibly converted to Islam after spending some years as a galley slave. He rose from slave to part owner of a brigantine, to galley owner, to Chief Admiral, to Administrator to the island of Samos, to Governor of Alexandria, to Pasha of Tripoli, to Beylerbey of Algiers, before dying in no doubt well-contented retirement in Istanbul. He is buried at the Kılıç Ali Pasha Mosque (1580), which he commissioned from the architect Mimar Sinan, and which is named in his honour (Uluç changed his name after becoming Beylerbey).

Antwerp Saved

DATE 1583, CENTURY VI, QUATRAIN 83

"Celuy qu'aura tant d'honneur & caresses,
A son entrée de la Gaule Belgique:
Un temps apres fera tant de rudesses,
Et sera contre à la fleur tant bellique."

He who will enjoy so many honours and endearments
On his entry into Belgian Gaul
Will, a while later, become so harsh
And be against the warlike flower.

This stunningly accurate quatrain describes the attempted sacking – under the aegis of the "French Fury" – of the Belgian city of Antwerp, on 15 January 1583 (*see* index date). François, Duke of Anjou (youngest son of Henri II and Catherine de Medici), was first invited into the United Provinces as hereditary sovereign in 1579, before being finally welcomed by William the Silent into Flushing in 1582. His powers, however, were limited through lack of public acclamation, and, being a proud fellow, François decided to take Antwerp, Bruges, Dunkirk and Ostend by force to cement his position. Attempting a joyous entry (i.e. "flower" pelted) into Antwerp, François and his invading force found themselves pelted with stones, logs, rocks, and chains instead. François escaped with a few men, leaving the rest – some say 1,500 – to be hacked to death by his enraged Belgian subjects. A truly remarkable quatrain, then, date perfect, and correct in every detail, depicting François, Duke of Anjou's, disastrously "un-triumphal" entry into Antwerp – followed by his unanticipated ejection.

Dutch Courage

DATE 1583, CENTURY X, QUATRAIN 83

"De batailler ne sera donné signe,
Du parc seront contraint de sortir hors,
De Gand lentour sera cogneu l'ensigne,
Qui fera mettre de tous les siens à mors."

No warning is given of the battle
They are forced out of the park
A banner is seen around Ghent belonging
To one who will kill all his own people.

A further description of François, Duke of Anjou's, disastrous attempt at sacking Antwerp. The so-called sacking rebounded on François, who abandoned 1,500 of his own men to the mob, becoming, in Nostradamus's perfect summing-up, "one who will kill all his own people". François failed to achieve a single one of his political ends, and he died a year later of malaria, more or less reconciled to his mother, Catherine de Medici, who had written to him after the debacle in the following terms: "Would that you had died young, for in that case you would not have been responsible for the death of so many fine gentlemen." His mother's wish came eerily true, for François was just 29 years old at the time of his death. "Ghent", which Nostradamus mentions in line three, was on the direct route taken by the French army into Antwerp, and so would certainly have seen François's "banners" passing by. "No warning" was indeed "given of the battle", for François had tricked the whole thing out as a joyous entry parade.

Gunpowder Plot

DATE 1605, CENTURY V, QUATRAIN 5

"Soubz umbre saincte d'oster de servitude,
Peuple & cité l'usurpera luy mesme:
Pire fera par fraulx de ieune pute,
Livré au champ lisant le faulx proesme."

Under the saintly shadow of slavery's overthrow
Both the people and the city will take matters into their own hands
He will do worse, thanks to the perfidy of the young whore
He will be delivered to the field reading the wrong poem.

There's an exquisite Nostradamian pun in the last line of this quatrain with *"livré"*, meaning delivered or sent, and *livre*, meaning book – a *jeux d'esprit* which blends in seamlessly well with "reading" and "poem". The poem in question must of course be *"Remember, remember, the fifth of November, / The gunpowder, treason and plot, / I know of no reason / Why gunpowder treason / Should ever be forgot"*, for the index date takes us directly to 5 November 1605, and the infamous Gunpowder Plot, in which James I and the entire English Protestant

ascendancy were due to be blown up by 36 barrels (i.e. 1,800 lbs) of gunpowder hidden beneath the Houses of Parliament. Guy Fawkes, who had had prior experience of explosives, was detailed to set the fuses and martyr himself for the Catholic cause. Before he was able to do so he was betrayed and captured, and then, by direct order of the king, progressively tortured, until he agreed to name names. He escaped the worst part of his punishment, however, by leaping off the scaffold at St Paul's Yard ("delivered to the field") and breaking his own neck, mere minutes before he was due to be hanged, drawn and quartered. The "young whore" may be taken symbolically to mean Lord Mounteagle, who, having originally sided with the plotters, is now believed to have contrived the letter giving the plotters away 11 days before the event was due to take place. The "young whore" aspect of the quatrain clearly refers to the fact that the 30-year-old Mounteagle received a stipend of £700 a year from the Crown for effectively averting the disaster. A fine quatrain, then, depicting the Catesby Gunpowder Plot and the attempted "saintly" (i.e. Roman Catholic) "overthrow" of the English Protestant ascendancy.

Glorious Revolution

DATE 1688–89, CENTURY IV, QUATRAIN 89

"Trente de Londres secret conjureront,
Contre leur Roi sur le pont l'entreprise:
Lui, fatalistes la mort degousteront,
Un Roi esleu blonde, natif de Frize."

Thirty Londoners will conspire in secret
Against their king; this to be undertaken by sea
He, and various fatalists, are disgusted by death
A blond king is elected, who was born in Friesland.

Anyone doubting Nostradamus's uncanny historical prescience has only to look at this quatrain, first published in 1557, and dealing, in detail, with events occurring up to 130 years later. The "blond king born in Friesland" is the Saxon William of Orange, who was formally invited to take England's crown by 29 signatories (with the Immortal Seven taking the lion's share of the credit, but with the actual number significantly closer to Nostradamus's "thirty"). William was to sail up the Thames with his fleet and take over the English throne in the name of his wife Mary (James II's daughter) and his mother Mary Stuart (eldest daughter of Charles I). James II and his commander-in-chief, John Churchill (later 1st Duke of Marlborough) are the "fatalists, disgusted by death" in line three, and it was James's decision to run rather than to fight, and John Churchill's decision to take his troops over to William at dead of night rather than to serve an unpopular king, that made the Glorious Revolution of 1688 a bloodless one, also.

French Revolution

DATE 1789, CENTURY X, QUATRAIN 89

"De brique en marbre seront les murs reduits
Sept et cinquante annees pacifiques,
Joie aux humains renoué Laqueduict,
Santé, grandz fruict joye et temps melifique."

The walls of small residences will go from brick to marble
Seven and fifty peaceful years
Joy to all humans, and the aqueduct ["that which was said"] renewed
Health, fruitfulness, joy and honeyed times.

We must take the word *"reduits"* exactly as written – in Old French it means a small house or habitation, rather than the more customary "reduced" (particularly when related to "bricks and marble"). This relatively minor change then provides us with a major key to the quatrain, which seems to lie in the concept of equality – i.e. on this day even small houses will be built to the same standards as palaces, and "all humans" (and not merely the elite) will know joy. Now to the index date of 89. And where does that take us? Why, to the exact start of the French Revolution and to the fall of the Bastille, on 14 July 1789, symbols of an uprising designed to achieve exactly the *Liberté, Égalité, Fraternité*, delineated in Nostradamus's quatrain. What then happens if we add 1789 to the "seven and fifty peaceful years" mentioned in line two? We come to 1846, and the escape of Louis Napoleon from the fortress of Ham – an event which led directly to the February Revolution of 1848.

Flight to Varennes

DATE 1791, CENTURY IX, QUATRAIN 20

"De nuit viendra par la forest de Reines,
Deux pars vaultorte Herne la pierre blanche,
Le moyne noir en gris dedans Varennes
Esleu cap. cause tempeste feu, sang tranche."

At night, via the forest, two Royals will come
Two couples, by mistake, the queen as white as a stone
The king as a grey-cowled monk in Varennes:
Anointed leader, he is the cause of the storm, fire, blood, slicing.

This justly famous quatrain describes the flight of Louis XVI and his queen, Marie-Antoinette, from Paris, by night, through the "royal forest" to "Varennes". "*La forest de Reines*" has a double meaning in this context, with *de Reines*, taken euphonically, giving "two Royals" or a "royal couple", something confirmed by Nostradamus's use of the Old French word *par* for a pair or couple in the very next line — "*de pars la roi*", for instance, also means "in the name of the king". The "pair" duly stopped for refreshment and a change of horses at Varennes, on 21 June 1791, where their disguise was instantly seen through, and they were taken into custody by the *procureur, cum* grocer, *cum* candle-maker, Monsieur Sauce (other sources ascribe the collar to the virulently Girondin postmaster of Sainte Menehould, Jean-Baptiste Drouet, who apparently recognized the king thanks to his appearance on French banknotes). Either way, it was clear that the royal pair were obviously not the servants of the Russian baroness (in reality the dauphin's governess, the Marquise de Tourzel) they and

their entourage claimed to be. Line two correctly describes the queen's fashionable "stone-white" hair and white dress (a giveaway, if ever there was one). The escape "by mistake" had been at the instigation of the queen, who was apparently frustrated at her husband's post-traumatic inanition following an attack on the Palace of Versailles by an angry mob. The use of the word "*tranche*" in line four presumably refers to the slicing action of the guillotine that was to cost the royal pair their lives less than two years later. A wonderfully prescient quatrain, then, describing the doomed flight of King Louis XVI and his wife, Marie-Antoinette, to Varennes, on 21 June 1791.

Fascisti Expelled

DATE 1922, CENTURY V, QUATRAIN 22

"Avant qu'à Rome grand aye rendu l'ame,
Effrayeur grande à l'armee estrangiere:
Par Esquadrons, l'embusche pres de Parme,
Puis les deux roges ensemble feront chere."

Before the great one of Rome gives up the ghost
There is a great uproar, thanks to an alien army
An ambush by squadrons near Parma
Then the two red ones will feast together.

"**P**arma" has had a chequered history, with Farneses and Bourbons galore, but the index date of 22 carries us out of the medieval era and into modern times. In August 1922, Parma became the first Italian city to resist Mussolini's *Fascisti*, when one of its Blackshirt officers, Italo Balbo (later governor general of Libya and heir apparent to Mussolini), attempted to enter the Oltretorrente quarter with his Celibano militia ("the alien army"). The local people formed themselves into the *arditi del populo* (the people's militia) and ambushed the incomers. The *squadristi* ("squadrons") were repulsed, and the "reds" celebrated, just as Nostradamus describes – red being the traditional colour of both the Italian communists and their anti-fascist allies, and also of Garibaldi's revolutionary *camicie rosse*, or red shirts. A splendid quatrain, date and detail perfect, showing the first organized resistance against the *Fascisti*, in Parma, in 1922 – the same year in which that great humanitarian, Pope Benedict XV, died unexpectedly of pneumonia ("before the great one in Rome gives up the ghost").

The Anschluss

DATE 1933, CENTURY III, QUATRAIN 33

"En la cité où le loup entrera,
Bien pres de là les ennemis seront:
Copie estrange grand païs gastera.
Aux murs & Alpes les amis passeront."

In the city which the wolf enters
There, nearby, will the enemy be
A foreign army will swallow the great country
Friends will cross both walls and Alps.

Given the index date of 33, this is clearly about Adolf Hitler's long-term plans for Austria, facilitated by German Federal elections on 5 March 1933, when Hitler's National Socialists won 44 per cent of the vote. Following Austrian Chancellor Engelbert Dolfuss's panic-stricken decision to suspend parliament and give himself dictatorial powers, the inevitable pro-Nazi riots broke out in Vienna, predating a virtual civil war. Dolfuss was assassinated on 25 July 1934 by eight home-grown Nazis intent on a coup, and, after numerous other outrages, Austria was duly annexed by – or merged with – Germany's Third Reich (depending on your point of view) four years later. The *Anschluss* followed an extensive *Heim in Reich* campaign, in which Hitler tried to persuade any person of German extraction still living outside Germany that their country should be part of a Greater Germany. A clear, concise, and index-date-perfect quatrain highlighting the seemingly inevitable merger between Austria and Germany in the already inflammatory environment of the 1930s.

May '68 Riots

DATE 1968, CENTURY X, QUATRAIN 67

"Le tremblement si fort au mois de May,
Saturne, Caper, Iupiter, Mercure au beuf:
Venus aussi Cancer, Mars, en Nonnay,
Tombera gresse lors plus grosse qu'un euf."

The powerful agitation in the month of May
Saturn in Aries, Jupiter, Mercury in Taurus
Venus and also Cancer, Mars, in Virgo
Sleet will fall, larger than an egg.

Nostradamus is one year out here (*see* index date), but when dealing with an event that happened 402 years after his death, that can hardly be accounted a failure, surely? We are talking, of course, of the May 1968 riots in Paris. The real start of the riots probably occurred on 6 "May", when the French student union, the UNEF (*Union Nationale des Étudiants de France*), together with the Union of University Teachers, called on their members to go out into the streets and protest against the police presence at the Sorbonne. A riot ensued, with barricades manned, and paving stones ("sleet will fall, larger than an egg") being hurled at the police. I drew up an astrological chart for two o'clock in the afternoon (being the time when the violent fighting began) on 6 May 1968, and discovered that "Saturn" was indeed in "Aries", with "Mercury" and "Venus" in "Taurus", just as Nostradamus predicts in lines two and three – in terms of planetary aspects, "Venus" was harmonizing with the ascendant planet "Virgo" (*see* line three), with "Jupiter" challenging "Mercury". Only "Cancer" is notable by its

absence. An excellent quatrain, then, and astrologically sound, with the month dead on, and the index date only a single year out, describing the May 1968 riots in Paris – an event that arguably changed the face of Europe by persuading democratic governments that they refuse to listen to the people's voice at their peril. The "powerful agitation" that Nostradamus describes in line one effectively describes a crucial period that saw not only the world's first wildcat strikes, but also the largest ever general strike – it boasted eleven million adherents – to actually succeed in stopping an advanced industrialized country dead in its tracks.

ENSLAVEMENT, EXPANSION and EMPIRE

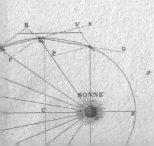

Ali Pasha

DATE 1571, CENTURY IV, QUATRAIN 92

"Teste tranchee du vaillant capitaine,
Sera getté devant son adversaire:
Son corps pendu de sa classe à l'antenne,
Confus fuira par rames à vent contraire."

The valiant captain's head is sliced off
It will be thrown in front of his adversary
His body will be hung on the yardarm in front of his fleet
They will retreat in confusion, oars against the wind.

This has to be about Sunday 7 October 1571's Battle of Lepanto, which saw the Ottoman navy, under Admiral Ali Pasha, engage the Holy League fleet, under Don John of Austria, at the northern end of the Gulf of Patras – the last major engagement in history to pit rowing vessels, in the form of galleys and galleasses ("oars against the wind") against each other. With the battle starting to turn against them, the Ottoman flagship, the *Sultana*, collided with the Holy League flagship, *La Real*, creating an indissoluble tangle of rigging. The two ships then became a battlefield, with the *Sultana* boarded, and Janissaries and Christians fighting each other with arquebuses (muskets), bows, cutlasses and scimitars. Twice, the Spanish *tercios* were repulsed, but on the third attempt they broke through, killing and beheading Ali Pasha, despite Don John's direct orders to the contrary. The head was then displayed to Don John ("it will be thrown in front of his adversary"), who, despite his initial qualms, then decided that he would be missing a trick if he didn't respond to

the good fortune that had so conveniently rolled his way. Ali Pasha's head was consequently speared onto a pike and hoisted high up on the "yardarm" of the Spanish flagship, sowing consternation in the Ottoman fleet ("they will retreat in confusion") and destroying Turkish morale. The main bulk of the Ottoman fleet, comprising 230 galleys, was either sunk or captured by the close of the engagement, with the Christian fleet losing no more than 15 galleys, and only half as many men as the Turks. Pope Pius V later claimed to have received news of this greatest of Christian victories via divine intervention, at the exact moment of Ali Pasha's death.

The British Empire I

"Le grand empire sera par Angleterre,
Le pempotam des ans plus de trois cens:
Grandes copies passer par mer et terre,
Les Lusitains n'en seront pas contens."

The greatest empire will be that of England
Plenipotentiary for more than three hundred years
Vast armies will move across sea and land
The Lusitanians will not be best pleased.

This may, on the surface, seem a straightforward quatrain – England to have the "greatest of all empires". So what's new about that? But this quatrain was published in 1568, at a time when England was still a relatively minor power. Suffice it to say that the quatrain is magnificently prescient, with an index date of 1600 giving us the granting of a royal charter by Queen Elizabeth I to the British East India Company, acknowledged by many as the world's first multinational corporation, and destined to be the symbolic and commercial bedrock of empire for the next 258 years. This certainly "displeased the Lusitanians", ergo the Portuguese and Spanish. Despite numerous ups and downs during its "more than three hundred years" of history, by 1921 the British Empire incorporated a quarter of the world's population and a quarter of the world's landmass. Termed the empire upon which the sun never set, it was certainly true that at any given time the sun would be shining on at least one of Britain's panoply of overseas territories.

Moorish Expulsions

DATE 1609, CENTURY I, QUATRAIN 9

"De l'Orient viendra le coeur punique
Facher Adrie, et les hoirs Romulides,
Acompaigné de la classe Libycque,
Trembler Mellites: et proches isles vuides."

From the east will come a Punic heart
To anger Hadrian and the heirs of Romulus [ides]
Accompanied by the Libyan fleet
The Melillans will tremble: neighbouring islands will empty.

In 16th-century France a "Punic heart" would have been taken to imply treachery (after Hannibal's breaking of a Roman treaty by crossing the Ebro) – but the pun, too, of "the punished heart" (*coeur puni*) might also be incorporated. The mention of the Roman Emperor "Hadrian" further reinforces the treachery motif, as Hadrian was believed by many to have murdered his predecessor, Trajan, with the connivance of Trajan's wife, Plotina. So we are left with an index date of 9, together with treachery from the east. This ties in perfectly with the final expulsion, on 22 September 1609, of the Moors and the Moriscos from Spain, on the jumped-up pretext that they had been in contact with the Turkish Empire (the "*classe Libycque*" – the main ports of the Barbary pirates were in Tripoli and Tunis), and were no doubt busy preparing an invasion. During the next five years 300,000 Moors crossed the Mediterranean into the Maghreb (and almost inevitably through "Melilla", which had been conquered by the Spanish in 1497, having originally been a "Punic" colony).

Fall of the Valois

DATE 1610, CENTURY I, QUATRAIN 10

"Serpens transmis dens la caige de fer
Ou les enfans septains du Roy sont pris:
Les vieux & peres sortiront bas de l'enfer,
Ains mourir voir de son fruict mort & crys."

The serpent uses its teeth in the iron cage
Where the king's seven children are held
The old men & fathers will emerge from hell's lower depths
Nay lamenting & dying to see their descendants dead.

Nostradamus was fond of the word *"caige"*, and he uses it often. In this case the connection would seem to be with the *caige d'or* from quatrain 1/35 – 1559 about Henri II of France, which describes the golden helmet of the unfortunate king whose visor was pierced by the shredded tip of Count Montgomery's lance during the course of what was designed to be nothing more than a friendly joust – a joust which went horribly, and irremediably, wrong. The king's unanticipated death effectively changed the history of France, and contributed to the

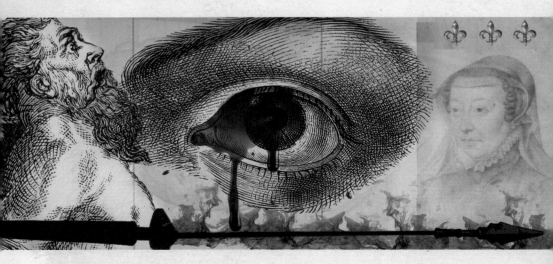

fall of the House of Valois. This was exemplified by the transfer of the remains of the last Valois king, Henri III, to the family mausoleum at Saint Denis in 1610 (*see* index date). Further proof of the Valois connection lies in the "seven children" mentioned in line two. Henri II and his wife, Catherine de Medici, had seven children, most of whom died young. They were, in order of age, Francis II (1543–60), Elisabeth (1545–68), Claude (1547–75), Charles IX (1550–74), Henri III (1551–89), Marguerite (1553–1615), and Hercules (1554–84). A third connection lies in the "serpent" metaphor in line one, for Catherine's nickname was *Madame Le Serpent* (The Snake Lady), based on her heraldic emblem (which she adopted after Henri II's death), and which depicted a snake with its tail in its mouth. This is a quatrain depicting the final fall from grace of the noble French House of Valois, therefore – an eventuality aided and abetted by the strictures of Salic law (which prohibited inheritance by the female sex), and which as good as handed control of France to the Bourbons, thanks to their line of descent from Louis IX (Saint Louis).

The British Empire II

DATE 1642/1942, CENTURY X, QUATRAIN 42

"Le regne humain d'Anglique geniture,
Fera son regne paix union tenir,
Captive guerre demi de sa closture,
Long temps la paix leur fera maintenir."

The humane reign will come from England
It will hold in peace and union
Half of what it encloses will have been captured by war
For a long time they will maintain the peace.

It's surprising how many of Nostradamus's verses deal with England. Given the tenor of quatrain 10/100 – 1600 (British Empire I), it is clear that Nostradamus believed that Britain, and not France, would end up by dominating the world for more than 300 years. Here he extends and broadens that prediction, giving us 42 as his index date. This presents us with a dilemma, for both 1642 and 1942 represent critical dates in the formation and eventual dissolution of the British Empire. Crucially, 1642 was a year which marked the formal beginnings of the First English Civil War, and, indirectly – via the eventual restitution of the Stuarts in the form of Charles II – to the inception of the British Empire. By 1942, on the other hand, it had become obvious that Britain, while not yet having reached its absolute nadir, was definitely on the way down as a world power. By terming the British Empire a "humane" one, Nostradamus seems to be asking his readers to concentrate on the British Empire's unifying, rather than on its colonizing, aspects.

Battle of Blenheim

DATE 1704, CENTURY X, QUATRAIN 4

"Sus la minuict conducteur de l'armee
Se saulvera, subit esvanouy,
Sept ans apres la fame non blasmee,
A son retour ne dira oncq ouy."

At the stroke of midnight the army commander
Will save himself, vanishing suddenly
Seven years later, his fame still unblemished
They will be all for his return.

John Churchill, 1st Duke of Marlborough (1650–1722), was the most consummate military genius that England ever produced. A staunch Anglican, he turned against his former master James II following the abrupt arrogation of his command to the Earl of Feversham, during the Monmouth Rebellion of 1685. Already a friend of William of Orange, Marlborough later deserted in the dead of night ("at the stroke of midnight") to William's cause during the so-called Glorious Revolution of 1688 (*see* 4/89: Glorious Revolution), thus "saving himself", and ensuring the continuation of what was to become a stupendous military career. The Duke of Marlborough's greatest battle was the Battle of Blenheim on 13 August 1704, in which he defeated Marshal Tallard's stronger army through the use of enlightened feint, resulting in over 30,000 French and Bavarians killed or wounded, with 11,000 French surrendering. Marlborough became the toast of England, with the likes of Joseph Addison writing him encomiums. He was later to be awarded Blenheim Palace for his pains.

War of Independence

DATE 1775, CENTURY IV, QUATRAIN 75

"Prest à combatre fera defection,
Chef adversaire obtiendra la victoire:
L'arrieregarde fera defention,
Les deffaillans mort au blanc territoire."

The one ready to fight will defect
The opposing leader will be victorious
The rearguard will defend itself
Defaulters will die in the white territory.

This quatrain is about the American War of Independence, and one of its most famous sons, Paul Revere. Having fought on the side of the British in the Seven Years' War, the ex-Huguenot Revere (originally Rivoire) switched his allegiance ("the one ready to fight will defect") to the Sons of Liberty and the Independent cause. Revere made his famous ride to Lexington on 16 April 1775 (*see* index date), to warn rebel leaders John Hancock and Samuel Adams that the British were coming to arrest them. This act predated the start of the American Revolution by two days, and Nostradamus correctly points up the first British victory at Bunker Hill on 17 June ("the opposing leader will be victorious"), together with a coded comment on the exact location of the battle, which took place on Breed's Hill (i.e. "white territory", taken from the Indians). A fine quatrain, then, detailing the events that led up to the start of the American War of Independence, together with the serpentine course the first few months of the conflict took.

US Independence

DATE 1776, CENTURY I, QUATRAIN 76

"D'un nom farouche tel proferé sera,
Que les trois seurs aurant fato le nom:
Puis grand peuple par langue et faict duira [dira]
Plus que nul autre aura bruit et renom."

His given name may seem a savage one
But both name and destiny were predicted by the three sisters
Following which a great people, through faith and language, will endure
His fame and his renown will surpass all others.

The "savage seeming name" belongs to Thomas Paine, born to impoverished parents in Thetford, Norfolk, and later to become the intellectual progenitor of the American Revolution through his publication, in 1776, of the pro-independence monograph *Common Sense*. The pamphlet sold 500,000 copies in the six months following its publication, proving instrumental in the drafting of the *Declaration of Independence* and in fomenting an *open* rather than a *concealed* movement towards the American colonies' eventual fracture with the mother country. The "three sisters" (as well as suggesting the three Fates) are probably those of Elizabeth Monroe (*la belle Americaine*), wife of James Monroe (American Minister to France and later fifth US President), who nursed Paine back to health after his 11-month custody in the Luxembourg Prison (he had fallen foul of Robespierre, and James Monroe had won his release). The last lines are self-evident, and deal with the influence on world events which Paine's concept of the US, and its *Lingua Franca*, English, have contrived.

Battle of the Nile

DATE 1798, CENTURY I, QUATRAIN 98

"Le chef qu'aura conduit peuple infini
Loing de son ciel, de meurs & langue estrange:
Cinq mil en Crete & Thessale fini,
Le chef fuiant sauvé en marine grange."

The chief who will have led the infinite people
Far from their own skies, towards strange customs and languages
Five thousand are finished in Crete and Thessaly
The fleeing leader escapes in a grain ship.

The "infinite people" was one of Nostradamus's favourite euphemisms for the French, and the index date of 98 takes us straight to Napoleon's 1798 Egyptian campaign ("far from their own skies, towards strange customs and languages"). The run-up to the Battle of the Nile (a.k.a. the Battle of Aboukir Bay), saw Napoleon, on his flagship *The Orient*, with 13 ships of the line, 4 frigates, and 280 subsidiary vessels, investing Crete on his way to Egypt ("Thessaly/ Iannina", under Ali Pasha, had become an ally after the 1797 Treaty of Camp Formio). With the French army ashore, and the fleet anchored, Nelson took the initiative and ordered an immediate attack ("Before this time tomorrow I shall have gained a peerage at Westminster Abbey"). Only 2 French ships of the line and 2 French frigates out of a total of 17 ships engaged managed to escape the ferocious British onslaught, but even these were later captured, leading to a total reversal of the Mediterranean status quo. The battle was a disaster for the French and a triumph for Admiral Nelson (despite the

occupational hazard of yet another wounding – this time Nelson was struck over his already blinded right eye, causing a flap of skin to fall across his face, temporarily blinding him). Napoleon was in Egypt with his army when he heard the news that between 2,000 and "5,000" of his men had been either killed or wounded in a battle that was to prove in many ways the precursor for the Battle of Trafalgar – for the future Admiral de Villeneuve (who was later to command French forces at Trafalgar in 1805) was one of the few initial escapees from the battleground (though he was subsequently captured in Malta).

Napoleon Crowned

DATE 1805, CENTURY IX, QUATRAIN 5

"Tiers doit du pied au premier semblera.
A un nouveau monarque de bas hault
Qui Pyse & Lucques Tyran occupera
Du precedant corriger le deffault."

The third toe will resemble the first
Of a new monarch, raised from low to high
The tyrant will occupy Pisa and Lucca
And will correct the faults of his predecessor.

This can surely only apply to Napoleon Bonaparte, who crowned himself emperor in Milan Cathedral on 26 May 1805 (*see* index date), using the iron crown of the ancient kings of Lombardy. Nostradamus describes Napoleon to a tee, with the emphasis on his having risen from "low to high" (Napoleon began as an artillery lieutenant and ended up as an emperor), and correctly points out that he "tyrannized" Italy, ending 1,000 years of Venetian independence and partitioning the country between France and Austria in the 1797 Treaty of Campo Formio. Nostradamus would probably have considered the Emperor Nero to be Napoleon's tyrannical predecessor, and his comment about Napoleon "correcting Nero's faults" may be taken as very much tongue-in-cheek, for it is, philosophically speaking, impossible for one tyrant to correct the faults of another for they are both, by definition, tyrants. A brilliant, date-perfect quatrain, then, punning nicely on the "toe" of Italy, and relating one tyrant (and owner of the toe) to another – Nero and Napoleon (both considered Antichristian by some).

Battle of Trafalgar

DATE 1805, CENTURY IV, QUATRAIN 5

"Croix, paix, soubz un accompli divin verbe,
L'Hespaigne & Gaule seront unis ensemble.
Grand clade proche, & combat tresacerbe:
Coeur si hardi ne sera qui ne tremble."

The cross, peace, under one perfect divine word
Spain and France united
A great disaster is imminent, and very bitter fighting
Even the hardiest heart will tremble.

Given the index date of 5 and the unlikely phrase "Spain and France united", this quatrain must be about the 1805–07 War of the Grand Alliance (as opposed to the countless other wars of the Grand Alliance), which united a powerful France, under Napoleon Bonaparte, and a weak Spain, under Charles IV, against the Third Coalition of England, Portugal, Russia and Austria. On 21 October 1805, Admiral Horatio Nelson defeated the combined French and Spanish fleet at the Battle of Trafalgar, destroying French naval power once and for all. There is a wonderful pun for all English speakers in line four, with the word "*hardi*", meaning "hardy" – for Nelson was shot by a French sharpshooter during the battle, and his dying words to his Flag Captain, Sir Thomas Hardy, were: "Kismet, Hardy." (Others would have it that Nelson said "Kiss me, Hardy", but that is unlikely, given the customs prevailing in the Royal Navy at that time). A superb quatrain about the pivotal Battle of Trafalgar, and the unlikely union between France and Spain.

Slavery Questioned

DATE 1814, CENTURY VII, QUATRAIN 14

"Faulx exposer viendra topographie,
Seront les cruches des monuments ouvertes:
Pulluler secte saincte philosophie,
Pour blanches, noires, et pour antiques vertes."

They will come and expose the false topography
The urns of the monuments will be opened
Sects, saints, and philosophy will pullulate
For whites, blacks, and ancient greens.

"*Faux*" is an interesting word, and can mean false or scythes. "*Cruches*", too, can mean either urns or fools. Nostradamus enjoys such ambivalences. The key to the quatrain, however, lies in line four, with the words "white" and "black". Given the index date of 14, and the "opening of monuments", the quatrain must refer to the destruction, by the British (under the aegis of the war of 1812) of Washington DC, the newly-formed capital of the United States (it was formally named in 1791). The destruction of Washington's

public buildings (the Senate, the Library of Congress, the House of Representatives and the United States Treasury in particular) was in revenge for the ravaging by the Americans of what are now the cities of Ontario and Toronto, following the Battle of York in 1813. At the time of the attack, Washington's population numbered 6,700 "whites", and 1,300 "blacks" – the first shot of the 1775 American Revolution ("the shot heard around the world") occurred, of course, at Lexington Green, and many of the earliest US Revolutionary flags were not, in fact, red, white, and blue, but "green" (*see* line four) to symbolize hope. Interestingly, after the end of the war, in 1815, John Quincy Adams (later to become the 6th US President) complained that British naval commanders had violated the terms of the Treaty of Ghent (which established the principle of *status quo ante bellum* – i.e. no new territorial concessions to be made by either side) by refusing to return American slaves captured during the war. This was a logical procedure on the part of the British, however, as they no longer recognized slaves as private property following the William Wilberforce-initiated United Kingdom Abolition of Slavery Act of 25 March 1807.

Simón Bolívar

DATE 1821, CENTURY IV, QUATRAIN 21

"Le changement sera fort difficile:
Cité, province au change gain fera:
Coeur haut, prudent mis, chassé lui habile.
Mer, terre, peuple son estat changera."

The change will be very difficult
Both the city and the province will profit by it
A great hearted man, prudently placed, will be forced to flee by a cunning one
Sea, land, and peoples – their condition will change.

The year 1821 was crucial for South America, and saw many changes, mostly for the better. The sequence began with Simón Bolívar's defeat of a Spanish army at Carabobo, triggering Venezuela and Ecuador's independence. A month later Peru declared independence under the "great-hearted" General José de San Martín, whose subsequent resignation in 1822, after a disagreement with the "cunning" and bulldozing *El Libertador* (Bolívar), allowed Bolívar to assume control of the country. San Martín was forced into exile ("forced to flee") in 1824, and died in Boulogne in 1850. Although Bolívar is almost endemically sanctified in South America to this day, many people consider San Martín the greater man. In September 1821, Guatemala, Honduras, El Salvador and Costa Rica all declared independence from Spain, with Panama following suit in December, when it merged with the province of Great Columbia. These changes had a profound effect on the future history of the whole of Latin America, making this one of Nostradamus's most successful and upbeat quatrains.

The Mahdi

DATE 1884/1885, CENTURY I, QUATRAIN 84

"Lune obscurecie aux profondes tenebres,
Son frère passe de couleur ferrugine:
Le grand caché long temps soubz les tenebres,
Tiedera fer dans la pluie sanguine."

The moon is hidden by deep shadows
Her brother, the sun, changes to the colour of blood
The great man is hidden by the shadows for a long time
They will warm their steel in the bloody rain.

The Mahdi and his band of Holy Warriors struggled to invest Khartoum between 12 March 1884 and 26 January 1885. Considered a "great man" by his followers, the Mahdi had retired to a cave ("the great man is hidden by the shadows") after his defeat before Omdurman, to await divine guidance from Allah. He returned with the news that Allah had declared 60 days of rest following which "blood would flow like water" – the Battle of Abu Klea, almost exactly 60 days later, was to prove him right. Nostradamus's mention of the "moon" in line one, and his reiteration of the word "shadows", further strengthens the Mahdi reading, as the moon, in the form of a crescent, was the symbol of Ottoman Islam. Thanks to perfidy on the part of General Gordon's Egyptian Lieutenant, Faraz Pasha, the gates of Khartoum were opened to the Mahdi's forces on 26 January 1885, and General Gordon was surprised on his way to the Austrian consulate, shot, and his head spitted on a spear and paraded around the city.

Fall of Khartoum

DATE 1885, CENTURY IV, QUATRAIN 85

"Le charbon blanc du noir sera chassé,
Prisonnier faict mené au tombereau:
More Chameau sur piedz entrelassez,
Lors le puisnay sillera l'aubereau."

The white charcoal will be driven out by the black
The prisoner is then ordered taken to the tumbril
The Moor's camel stands on intertwined feet
When the late-born one sews up the hawk's eyelids.

Line four may seem grotesque, but the action of "seeling" a hawk's eyelids – the word *siller*, in Old French specifically meant to "seel" in this manner – was a traditional part of the Eastern hawking tradition, requiring the falconer to sew the hawk's eyelids shut for a period of about one week, during which it was hoped that the bird would stop baiting and would begin to take meat from the hand. The mention of such a specific part of the Eastern hawking tradition reinforces the reading of "Moor", and "black" in the text – "white charcoal" exists too, of course, the only difference lying in the temperature of the charring, and the existence of a whitish hue that covers the surface of the charcoal as a result of the smothering powder (ergo the surface difference between a "white" and a "black" man). The index date of 85 then takes us directly to the 1885 Fall of Khartoum, when the Mahdi's troops succeeded in investing the city and killing General Gordon, commander of the British evacuation force.

Mahatma Gandhi

DATE 1930, CENTURY X, QUATRAIN 30

"Nepveu & sang du sainct nouveau venu,
Par le surnom soustient arcs & couvert
Seront chassez mis à mort chassez nu,
En ruge & noir convertiront leur vert."

Descendant and blood of the newly-arrived saint
Thanks to his surname he will sustain arches and shelter
They will be driven out, killed, stripped naked
Their green will change to red and black.

Mohandas Karamchand Gandhi (later known as the Mahatma, or Great Soul) began his campaign of nonviolent civil disobedience vis-à-vis the English, on 12 March 1930 (*see* index date). Within a year of his influential Salt March, 60,000 of his followers had been arrested for breaching the government monopoly on salt production, and further riots and massacres followed before India attained independence from the United Kingdom on 15 August 1947. "Their green" mentioned in line four, relates to the national colour of Pakistan, and the implication that it would change "to red and black" (the archetypal colours of blood and death) is a reference to the bloodshed occasioned by the disastrous partition of India, which Gandhi vehemently opposed and which his Muslim counterpart, Muhammad Jinnah, took as a sine qua non. A fine quatrain, depicting the early career of "the newly-arrived saint", Mahatma Gandhi, and his pivotal influence both on the culture and soul of India, and on the eventual emergence of his country as an independent, democratically driven, nation.

The Sparing of Aachen

DATE 1941, CENTURY VII, QUATRAIN 41

"Les oz des piedz & des main enserrés,
Par bruit maison long temps inhabitee:
Seront par songes concavant deterrés,
Maison salubre & sans bruyt habitee."

The bones of the feet and the hand are contained
For a long time, thanks to the noise, the house remains uninhabited
They are disinterred by hollow dreams
The healthy and peaceful house is inhabited once again.

The Emperor Charlemagne (742–814), founding father of both France and Germany, and considered by many to be the true father of Europe, established Aachen (Aix-La-Chapelle) as his *Roma Secunda* (second Rome), intending it to form the major part of his *renovatio imperii Romanorum* (revival of the Roman Empire) project. In consequence, the imperial palace at Aachen was built on a grandiose scale, and was designed to attract artists, musicians, theologians, scholars and poets to the court of this great Frankish king. If you leave the cathedral today and walk to the end of the street and turn immediately right, you will come to the great treasury of Aachen Cathedral, housing the famous "relics" which Nostradamus mentions in line one. One of the primary relics (the mortal remains of saints, etc., as opposed to objects merely connected with them) is known as the Arm Reliquary, and is constructed in the form of an upraised "hand" – the hand that held Charlemagne's famous sword *Joyeuse*, or "joyful", which was buried with its owner – and within which the

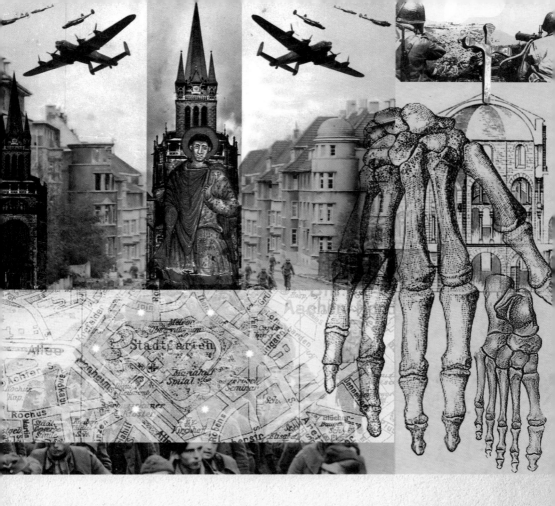

ulna and radius of Charlemagne's right forearm can be clearly seen behind a rock-crystal pane of glass. Due to the symbolic importance of Aachen to European sensibilities, it was decided, during the Second World War, that the cathedral would be specifically spared during bombing raids. To this end pathfinders were sent ahead to mark its precincts, and the (largely British) bombing crews effectively avoided destroying what Nostradamus tellingly calls the "house" (of Europe). On 21 October 1944 there was a massive German surrender at Aachen, which finally restored the peace so tellingly described by Nostradamus in line four, ending, once and for all, Adolf Hitler's "hollow dreams".

Guantanamo Bay

DATE 2002, CENTURY I, QUATRAIN 59

"Les exilez deportés dans les isles
Au changement d'ung plus cruel monarque
Seront meurtrys: & mis deux des scintiles,
Qui de parler ne seront estés parques."

The exiles are deported to the islands
When the new leader proves even crueller
There are murders; two at a time they will be questioned
Until they cannot stop speaking.

More than 500 political detainees were transferred from Camp X-Ray to the newly built Camp Delta at Guantanamo Bay (which forms part of the Cuban archipelago, ergo "the islands") following the so-called defeat of the Taliban in Afghanistan in 2002. After the US/Iraq war of 2003, even more "exiles" were transferred there. In Ba'athist terms, President Bush would no doubt have been perceived as an even "crueller" leader than Saddam Hussein, and countless "murders" have been committed as a result of US intervention in both countries. The Bush regime, embarrassed by bad publicity over its treatment of the internees, later struggled to establish a legally viable argument to justify its harsh interrogation techniques at Guantanamo, which, as one US official dryly commented at the time, is the "legal equivalent of outer space". It is reasonable to suppose that prisoners, on the receiving end of such techniques, would often talk "until they cannot stop speaking". Despite concerted protests and sustained media attacks, Guantanamo Bay was still in existence at the time of writing.

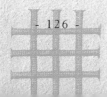

US/Iraq War I

"De feu volant la machination,
Viendra troubler au grand chef assigés:
Dedans sera telle sedition,
Qu'en desespoir seront les profligés."

The contrivance of flying fire
Will come to trouble the besieged leader
Inside, there will be so much sedition
That the corrupt ones will despair.

This has a clear connection with 6/97 – 2003: US/Iraq War II, with its use of the "flying fire" and "burning sky" analogies, together with the implication of a "besieged" city, and its embattled leader. It is saying, in essence, that Saddam Hussein will be attacked from the sky. His own people will rise against him. He will belatedly recognize the mistakes he has made, but it will be too late to change the outcome of the attack. By the end of his 24-year hold on power, Saddam Hussein had indeed become completely "corrupt", and his autocracy knew, quite literally, no bounds. It is also perfectly possible to read line one's "contrivance of flying fire" as implying that Hussein would encounter problems with weapons of mass destruction, and that these would contribute to his downfall. We do know that he viciously put down all "sedition" within the ranks of his Ba'athist party, even going so far as to have members of his own immediate family killed for disloyalty. All these factors make the quatrain particularly impressive.

US/Iraq War II

DATE 2003, CENTURY VI, QUATRAIN 97

"Cinq & quarante degrés ciel bruslera,
Feu approucher de la grand cité neufve,
Instant grand flamme esparse saultera,
Quant on voudra des normans faire preuve."

The sky will burn those at 45 degrees
Fire will approach the great new city
All of a sudden a thick wall of flame will leap upwards
When they ask for proof from the Northerners.

"**45** degrees" north runs pretty much plumb through the centre of Baghdad, which might indeed, in 2003, have been construed as "the great new city", given the enormous amount of building work undertaken, following the Gulf War of 1991, at the behest of the vainglorious Saddam Hussein. We know Nostradamus means the northern rather than the southern latitudes because of his mention of "*normans*", in line four, which was a common euphemism at the time for those from the north – the French have traditionally been, and still are, extremely fond of such wordplay. It is true that, for an unconscionably long time, Saddam Hussein, suffering no doubt from Dictator Denial Syndrome, believed that the US and their British and Australian allies ("the Northerners") would not attack Baghdad itself – rather as Hitler once believed that Britain would not declare war on Germany, and Stalin once believed that Hitler would honour the Nazi/Soviet non-aggression pact they he and his German allies had hatched between them as part of their efforts to partition Eastern

Europe. The US used what they called "shock and awe" tactics on 20 March, and great "walls of flame" ("the skies will burn") did indeed "leap upwards" from all around Baghdad city in a massive display of military firepower. The initial campaign was declared formally over by President Bush (somewhat prematurely with the benefit of hindsight) on 1 May 2003, paving the way for the much longer and more prickly transition towards a peaceful democracy (an ongoing process that had certainly not ended at the time of writing). The reason for Nostradamus's repeated use of the words "burn", "fire" and "flame" is self-evident to anyone who has seen footage of the conflict.

DISASTER, DISEASE and DESOLATION

Venice Plague	Twin Towers II
Russian Famine	Financial Meltdown
Great Fire of London	Planet in Peril
Twin Towers I	Drought & Floods

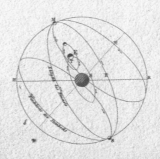

Venice Plague

DATE 1575, CENTURY VI, QUATRAIN 75

"Le grand pilot par Roy sera mandé,
Laisser la classe pour plus hault lieu attaindre:
Sept ans apres sera contrebandé,
Barbare armée viendra Venise craindre."

The great pilot is sent for by the king
He must leave the fleet for a higher post
He will be smuggled seven years later
A barbarian force will come to terrify Venice.

In 1575 the city of Venice was decimated by the bubonic plague (*yersinia pestis*). There is such a remarkable correlation between these events and Nostradamus's own index date, that it seems pointless to look further. Venice took extraordinary precautions to control the outbreak, including sealing up its port and isolating all ships to a nearby island. But smuggling abounded, and the plague made its way past the city's defences until fully 33 per cent of the population was stricken (nearly 50,000 people) during the period of nearly three years the plague took to wind down. At its worst, the only people walking the streets were the freakishly garbed plague doctors, and the *pizzicamorti* (the gravediggers), who, as well as wearing tarred cloaks, were also required to wear bells on their ankles to warn of their arrival ("a barbarian force will come to terrify Venice"). The Franciscan Church of the Redentore was built in 1577, on the island of Guidecca, to commemorate the event. The doge ("the great pilot") and all his senators attended its opening.

Russian Famine

DATE 1605, CENTURY VI, QUATRAIN 5

"Si grand famine par unde pestifère,
Par pluye longue le long du polle artique:
Samarobryn cent lieux de l'hemispere,
Vivront sans loy, exemp de pollitique."

There is such great famine thanks to a wave of pestilence
Great rains will fall over the Arctic pole
Brown Samara one hundred leagues from the hemisphere
They will live without law, and outside political control.

For some reason Nostradamian commentators have found great problems with the word "*Samarobryn*". My principle of euphonic translation works perfectly here, especially when twinned with the glaring clue of a "great famine". For "Samara" was founded in 1586 as both a defence outpost, and as the major grain-trading centre, of the Volga region, and *bryn*, of course, is merely the French euphonic pronunciation of *brun*, meaning brown, as in grain. Samara is indeed situated exactly 100 leagues (approx. 270 miles) from the "hemisphere" of the Caspian lowlands, and Russia did indeed suffer terrible "floods" and "famine" between 1601 and 1605 (*see* index date). The Dutch cartographer Isaac Massa (1586–1643) later wrote: "Even the famine described by Albert, Abbot of Stadten, could not be compared with this one; so great was the famine and poverty in Moskovia that even mothers ate their children. All roads were strewn with people who had died of famine, and their bodies were eaten by wolves, foxes, and other beasts. This lasted for 4 years, almost till 1605."

Great Fire of London

"Le sang du juste à Londres sera faute
Bruslez par fouldres de vingt trois les six.
La dame antique cherra de place haute:
De mesme secte plusieurs seront occis."

The blood of the upright will be absent from London
She will burn up suddenly by Divine Will in the year ending 666
The old lady will fall from her high place
Many other Protestant churches will be destroyed, too.

This stands as one of Nostradamus's greatest quatrains, describing the fire of London explicitly and without recourse to obfuscation. The "blood of the upright" may be taken to refer sardonically to the nobility, many of whom were quick to leave London – the king, of course, famously only learned of the full extent of the fire from Samuel Pepys's eyewitness account, brought to him in the comparative safety of Whitehall (although that, too, was threatened on the final day of the fire). Four fifths of the city was destroyed in the fire (13,200 houses, 50 livery halls, 87 churches, covering, in total, an area of 436 acres), which Nostradamus dates with total accuracy by multiplying 20 by 3 plus 6 = 66 (a literal reading of the original French at the end of line two gives us "of 20, 3, the 6"). A more specifically euphonic reading of the same line takes us even closer in date, with *bruslez par fouldres de vingt trois les* six being read as *bruslez par fouldres divin trois les six*

("burned by divine fires + three sixes") – with 666, of course, being the devil's number. The "old lady" in line three is St Paul's Cathedral, which was destroyed alongside 86 of the city's 109 churches ("*secte*", in line four, is the Catholic Nostradamus's way of telling us that these are Protestant churches going up in flames, for to the Catholic Church in Nostradamus's time, the Protestant Church was, most definitely, a sect). And to cap it all, the second line may also be read, if taken in an alternative euphonic way, as "*brulez par foudre divin, troyes, les six*" ("burned by divine lightning, like Troy, but only six died"). Only "six" people did die in the fire.

Twin Towers I

DATE 2001, CENTURY I, QUATRAIN 87

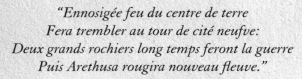

"Ennosigée feu du centre de terre
Fera trembler au tour de cité neufve:
Deux grands rochiers long temps feront la guerre
Puis Arethusa rougira nouveau fleuve."

Earthshaking, a fire from the centre of the earth
Will shake the towers of the new city
As a result, two great rocks will fight a long war
Until Arethusan springs bloody the river afresh.

An uncanny foretelling of the Twin Towers disaster, even down to a paralleling of the two rock-like towers with a war between the "two great rocks" of Christianity and Islam. The towers are brought down by "fire from the centre of the earth", an extraordinary leap of the imagination for Nostradamus when one bears in mind that the explosive catalyst used in the attacks was oil-based aviation fuel. Another extraordinary coincidence links the myth of "Arethusa" with her legendary springs at Ellis, to that of Ellis Island, which was for many years the main immigration gateway to New York. Nostradamus's use of the term *cité neufve* (the "New City"), immediately links 1/87 to the next quatrain in our series, 10/49 – 2001: Twin Towers II. Other similarities between the two also merit attention; the mention of rocks and mountains; the symbols of water and its poisoning, the first time with blood, the second with sulphur; and the Arethusan springs, at both Ellis and Syracuse (also a place in New York State), twinned with the "world's garden".

Twin Towers II

DATE 2001, CENTURY X, QUATRAIN 49

"Jardin du monde au pres de cité neufve,
Dans le chemin des montaignes cavees,
Sera saisi & plongé dans la Cuve,
Beuvant par force eaux soulfre envenimees."

The world's garden near the New City
In the roadway, hollow mountains,
They will be seized, and plunged into the sewers
People will be forced to drink the sulphur-poisoned waters.

A chilling image of the Twin Towers, which Nostradamus describes visually – and in the only way he is able, given the limitations of the period in which he is living – as "hollow mountains in the roadway". We already know, from 1/87 – 2001: Twin Towers I, that his "New City" is New York. Here he presents a terrifying picture of the two skyscrapers being "plunged into the sewers", descriptions that could have been taken direct from television news pictures of the disaster showing the towers crumpling inexorably earthwards. "Sulphur-poisoned waters" can be taken both figuratively and as a metaphor for the realization, by the United States, that from this moment on, they, too, are vulnerable, and that they will be forced to drain the chalice of poisoned water fate has handed them to its dregs. A précis of the quatrain would run as follows. The destruction of the Twin Towers will traumatize the people of the United States. There will be many long-term effects, and they will inevitably poison relations between the US and Islam.

Financial Meltdown

DATE 2008, CENTURY VIII, QUATRAIN 28

"Les simulachres d'or & argent enflez,
Qu'apres le rapt au lac furent gettez
Au desouvert estaincts tous & troublez.
Au marbre escript prescripz intergetez."

Fake versions of gold and silver multiply
Such that after the abduction they are thrown into the lake
On their rediscovery, global exhaustion and trouble
All debts are voided.

One has merely to glance through this quatrain, and at its century number of 8 and index date of 28, to realize that this is a categorical depiction of the 2008 world financial crisis, right down to Nostradamus's memorable phrase, "all debts are voided" (with its revocations of the US sub-prime mortgage debacle). The quatrain describes 2008's global financial meltdown to a tee, a credit crisis triggered by the use of artificial replacements for cash – i.e. credit cards, national debt, commodity speculation, hedge funds, and a

raft of other dubious financial instruments – just as Nostradamus predicts in his phrase "fake versions of gold and silver multiply". But that isn't the end of it. As well as abduction, *"rapt"* in line two can also be used in the sense of a rape. Following the rape of the financial markets, therefore, and the collapse of "fake" monetary objects, all debts between nation states are either "voided" or put on hold. It is the 79th year after the great 1929 Wall Street stock market crash, remember, a crisis which triggered the Great Depression of the 1930s – Nostradamus is clearly predicting another equally catastrophic event here. This time, however, he feels that the crash will mirror the collapse of spiritual values throughout the world, giving people nothing to cling on to in fraught times. That is surely the meaning of his phrase "global exhaustion" – the catastrophic loss of hope due to the crisis in religious faith he goes on to describe in a later index-date-connected quatrain, 2/28 – 2008: "The last but one holder of the prophet's name, / Will take Diana for his day and for his rest / He will wander far with his head in a frenzy / Delivering a great people from financial subjugation."

Planet in Peril

"Faulx à l'estang ioinct vers le Sagitaire
En son hault AUGE de l'exaltation,
Peste, famine, mort de main militaire:
Le siecle approche de renovation."

Scythes in the mill-run, joining towards Sagittarius
In it high mill-course of exaltation
Plague, famine, and death through war
The century approaches its remaking.

An early warning, by Nostradamus, of the wrong direction the world is taking. Using wheat and barley images from the Revelation of St John the Divine 6. vi., he cautions us that unless we attempt to mend our ways, the planet will be taken from us and remade in an image we may find uncongenial. "*Sagitaire*", in line one, represents Sagittarius the archer, and he is the horseman revealed at the opening of the First Seal by the beckoning of the first of the four beasts: "And I saw, and behold a white horse; and he that sat on him had a bow;" (Revelations 6. ii.). The upshot of the opening of the last of the Seven Seals is too abominable to contemplate, and we must take this quatrain as a warning about the damage we are doing to our planet and to its climate. God gave the planet to us as a gift, Nostradamus is saying, and, if we are not careful, He may take it back and remake it in a different image.

Drought & Floods

DATE 2017, CENTURY I, QUATRAIN 17

"Par quarante ans l'Iris n'apparoistra,
Par quarante ans tous les jours sera veu:
La terre aride en siccité croistra,
Et grans deluges quand sera aperceu."

For forty years the iris will not appear
For a further forty, it shall be seen every day
The already arid earth will grow still more parched
Great floods, when the iris is seen again.

In Old French *"l'Iris"* was both a rainbow and an iris – the first image is meant metaphorically, the second literally. "Iris" was the goddess of the rainbow, and she is the messenger of the gods when they intend discord, the rainbow being the bridge from heaven let down for her convenience in carrying her message. The "iris" flower is commonplace, and of no special significance except in its very banality. Nostradamus seems to be implying that if we have reached a stage in our treatment of the planet in which such a simple organism as a flower can no longer grow, then we have already reached crisis point. The last two lines are as clear a picture of global warming, followed by torrential flooding after the wholesale destruction of our moisture-holding forests, as we are ever likely to get. By 2017 the planet is clearly reaching crisis point, and we are in danger of losing much of the natural beauty that we now take for granted. Something must be done before it is too late.

HEROES,
HOLY MEN
and HIGH
HITTERS

John of the Cross	J.S. Bach
Kepler's Supernova	Voltaire
King James Bible	Charles Darwin
Nostradamus's Qualms	Albert Einstein
Duc de Saint-Simon	Scopes Monkey Trial
Antonio Stradivari	Berlin Olympics

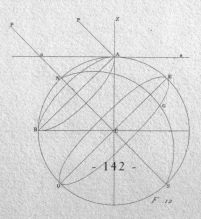

John of the Cross

DATE 1579, CENTURY V, QUATRAIN 79

"La sacree pompe viendra baisser les aesles
Par lavenue du grand legislateur:
Humble haulsera vexera les rebelles,
Naistra sur terre aucun aemulateur."

Sacred display will have its wings clipped
Thanks to the great legislator
He will raise up the humble and harry the rebels
He will be unique.

Given the index date of 79, and taking into account Nostradamus's Catholicism, his Jewish ancestry, and his mystical bent, there is only one possible candidate for the "great" man we are talking of here. Imprisoned and brutalized by his fellow Carmelites for attempting to reform monastic practice, Saint John of the Cross (Juan de Yepes Alvarez) was plunged into an existential crisis from which he emerged as the author of one of the world's supreme mystical masterpieces. In 1579 St John wrote his seminal poem *The Dark Night of the Soul*, which described the trials of a soul, stripped of its customary comforts and accoutrements, yet striving towards union with God. A hero of the Counter-Reformation (and, somewhat perversely, descending from a Jewish *converso* family), Saint John, together with Saint Teresa of Avila, founded the discalced Carmelites ("he will raise up the humble"), and is considered one of the supreme masters of Spanish literature. Canonized in 1762, Saint John is one of only 33 Doctors of the Church (those whose writings have imbued present faith).

Kepler's Supernova

DATE 1604, CENTURY III, QUATRAIN 4

"Quand seront proches le defaut des lunaires,
De l'un à l'autre ne distant grandement,
Froid, siccité, danger vers les frontieres,
Mesmes ou l'oracle a prins commencement."

When the lunar default is near
And one is not far from another
Cold, dryness, danger at the borders
Even where the oracle began.

"*L*unaire", as well as meaning lunar, also means moonwort in Old French (*Botrychium lunaria*). Moonwort is a fern, and was used by alchemists and physicians as a vulnerary herb (i.e. for the treatment of wounds), and also, on occasion, taken internally as a remedy for dysentery or ruptures. Nostradamus was very aware of the double meanings of words, and often used them on purpose. In this case he seems to be talking about a lunar eclipse, twinned with the failure of a course of healing treatment. Given the index date of 4, however, perhaps it was not of a lunar eclipse he was talking, but of the moon eclipsed by a brighter star? The answer to the conundrum lies in SN 1604, the last historical supernova to be seen in our galaxy. It was first noticed on 9 October 1604, in the constellation Ophiuchus. Copernican astronomer/astrologer Johannes Kepler later put the star under detailed observation. The supernova was already as bright as Mars, and went on to eclipse Jupiter in brightness a few days later.

King James Bible

DATE 1611, CENTURY III, QUATRAIN 11

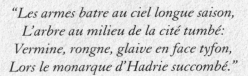

"Les armes batre au ciel longue saison,
L'arbre au milieu de la cité tumbé:
Vermine, rongne, glaive en face tyfon,
Lors le monarque d'Hadrie succombé."

Weapons clash in the sky for a long time
The tree in the centre of the city has fallen
Vermin, gnawing, a sword in Typhon's face
When the Hadrian king succumbs.

The giant "Typhon", with his 100 heads, scared the wits out of all the gods, causing them to transform into animals to escape his wrath. Zeus then pulled himself together at the very last moment and drove Typhon out of heaven with his thunderbolts ("weapons clash in the sky for a long time"), and Typhon ended up conveniently crushed beneath the slopes of Mount Etna. Is Nostradamus being guilty of wishful thinking here? Read on and decide for yourselves. Nostradamus's mention of a "Hadrian king" in line four gives us our next clue, and may be a coded suggestion of homosexuality, as Hadrian was notorious for his love of the young Bithynian youth, Antinous, whose death prompted Hadrian to turn him into a god with his very own Nile city, Antinopolis. Given the index date of 11, James I of England must be the obvious candidate for the "Hadrian king", thanks to his publicly proclaimed love for George Villiers, Duke of Buckingham ("the handsomest man in England"). The symbols of the "tree" and the "sword" then take on quite different connotations, and may be

being used by Nostradamus specifically to undermine James's position (remember Zeus versus Typhon?) as the progenitor of the Authorised Version. James's great Bible was completed in 1611 after the king had detailed 47 (originally 54) Church of England scholars to scrupulously translate and prepare – from original Greek, Hebrew and Aramaic texts – a specifically Protestant Bible (i.e. one conforming to Anglican ecclesiology and Episcopal dogma). The Bible's first appearance elicited horror from Catholics everywhere – just as it would have done from the ultra-Catholic Nostradamus – although later they would come to both accept and use it.

Nostradamus's Qualms

DATE 1627, CENTURY II, QUATRAIN 27

"Le divin verbe sera du ciel frappé,
Qui ne pourra proceder plus avant.
Du reserant le secret estoupé
Qu'on marchera par dessus & devant."

The diviner's word will be struck from the sky
He will not be able to go any farther into the future
The unlocker's secret is crippled
He will be trodden on from both the front and the back.

Most commentators, working from later editions of the *Centuries*, have assumed that the word in line one is *"divin"*, in the sense of divine – but they are not taking into account the context of the quatrain, and its subsidiary meaning. Nostradamus is talking about a *devin*, here, which in Old French means a diviner or conjuror – he is talking about himself, in other words. The word *"reserant"* in line three comes from the Latin *resero*, meaning to unlock, and *"estoupé"*, not a French word in itself, most probably comes from *estropié*, meaning a cripple or maimed person. The implication is one of fear, therefore – fear that a valued gift or other sign of grace may be withdrawn or prejudiced in some way. Nostradamus seems to be suggesting that, even if the gift of prophecy is not withdrawn specifically from him, that by 1627 (*see* index date), his predictions will be attacked from all sides, and that his revelations about the Church and the Crown would be hijacked or compromised in some way. He was right.

Duc de Saint-Simon

DATE 1659, CENTURY IX, QUATRAIN 59

"A la Ferté prendra la Vidame
Nicol tenu rouge qu'avoit produit la vie.
La grand Loyse naistra que fera clame.
Donnant Bourgongne à Bretons par enuie."

La Ferté will take Vidame
Nicolas, red-clothed, which has produced life
Great Louis will be born – he will be famous
Making both Burgundians and Bretons envious.

"La Ferté-Vidame" is a tiny village 39 kilometres to the west of Dreux, and about 120 kilometres west of Paris (a "vidame" traditionally commanded the military forces of a bishop). It has two famous "Louis" amongst its past inhabitants, one of whom, King Louis-Philippe I of France, made a brief visit there in 1846. Our second Louis has a far better claim to the quatrain, however, for he was the "great Louis" de Vouvroy, Duke of Saint-Simon and Pair de France (a title of the highest nobility), who wrote his "famous" memoirs at the "Chateau De La Ferté-Vidame", and who acted as godfather to many of his vassals at the Church of St "Nicolas" (*see* quatrain), an edifice that had been rebuilt by his father in the years 1659–60 (*see* index date). All these connections make of this a wonderful and eponymously exact quatrain depicting the great French memoirist Saint-Simon (1675–1755), whose posthumous influence extended far into the future, touching the likes of Marcel Proust (1871–1922), Count Leo Tolstoy (1828–1910), and Gustave Flaubert (1821–80).

Antonio Stradivari

DATE 1669, CENTURY VIII, QUATRAIN 69

"Aupres du jeune le vieux ange baisser
Et le viendra surmonter à la fin:
Dix ans esgaux au plus vieux rabaisser;
De trois d'eux l'un huitiesme seraphin."

The old angel bows before the younger one
But he will rise above him in the end
He is reduced to ten years of equality with the old one
Of the three of them, only one becomes the eighth seraph.

The "seraphim" are angels of light, and they reside directly in the presence of God. Each has six wings and four heads, and they may not be seen by human eyes. Their upper wings are used for flying, their middle wings cover their eyes, and their lower wings cover their feet or genitals. The seraphim are musical (they form part of the angelic choir, which constitutes the highest order in the hierarchy of angels), and one of their main duties is to sing the praises of the Lord (the Sanctus, or Trisagion), which they do using the words "Holy, holy,

holy, is the Lord of hosts: the whole earth is full of his glory" (Isaiah vi: 3 and Revelations iv: 8). This musical element is crucial in any reading of this complex quatrain, and, following the musical link, we duly find that the index date of 69 leads us to 1669, the year in which Antonio Stradivari (1644–1737), "touched by the hand of God", made his very first violin. Stradivari, then, is the "old angel", and Bartolomeo Guiseppe Guarneri del Gesù (1698–1744), his main rival, is the "younger one". The "old one" in line three is Nicolò Amati (1596–1684), who, at least according to his own contemporaries, was by far the greater violin maker, and was both Stradivari's teacher, and that of Guarneri's grandfather, Andrea. Nostradamus's image of Stradivari becoming the eighth seraph is a rather beautiful one, therefore, and no doubt reflects the master's ability to encapsulate light (*saraph* means "to burn") in the making of his musical instruments. There were about 1,100 instruments in all, including violins, violas, cellos, harps, and guitars – of which perhaps 650 still survive in playable condition to this day.

J.S. Bach

DATE 1695, CENTURY I, QUATRAIN 95

*"Devant moustier trouvé enfant besson,
D'heroic sang de moine et vestutisque:
Son bruit par secte langue et puissance son
Qu'on dira fort eleué le vopisque."*

**The son of a twin will be found in front of a monastery
Fruit of the heroic blood of a monk, and of ancient lineage
His fame will be known through Protestantism, tongue, and powerful sound
So that one might say that the survivor of this twin will indeed be raised high.**

The Bach family was of ancient Hungarian origin, and were so numerous, and of such high standing in the Thuringian community, that around Erfurt and Eisenach any musician eventually came to be known as a "Bach". The Bachs went on to produce seven generations of musicians, spanning in time from the age of Luther (who studied at the University of Erfurt, and became, famously, a "monk" at the Augustinian Erfurt Monastery), to that of Bismarck. The key to this quatrain lies in the concept of a "twin", and in the index date of 95. Put the two together, and one gets 1695, which is the year in which Johann Sebastian Bach's father, Johann Ambrosius, unexpectedly died, two years after his twin brother Johann Christoph, and less than a year after Bach's mother, Elisabeth Lämerhirt. During his lifetime, Bach became the musical conscience of German Protestantism, and this link between Martin Luther (the "monk" and the "monastery") and Johann Sebastian Bach (the "son of a twin" and the "fomenter of a powerful sound") cements the reading.

Voltaire

DATE 1726, CENTURY I, QUATRAIN 26

"Le grand du fouldre tumbe d'heure diurne,
Mal & predict par porteur postulaire
Suivant presaige tumbe d'heure nocturne,
Conflit Reims, Londres, Etrusque pestifère."

The great one falls to lightning during the daytime
Evil and the prediction borne by a competitor
According to the presage the fall of night
Will bring conflict to Reims, London, Etruscan plague.

Many puns here, with *"tumbe"* being only the most obvious – the word appears to be a composite of *tombe* (fall) and *tombeau* (tomb). This is reiterated by the "Etruscan plague", which presumably means to be extinguished like the Etruscan race, who are now only known about from the evidence found on their tombs. Given the index date of 26, and the extinguishing of a race (ergo the *ancien régime* and its inherited privileges), this quatrain stakes its claim to being about the great French philosopher François Marie Arouet (Voltaire), who fell foul of a member of the aristocracy (the Chevalier de Rohan) in 1726, and was bastinadoed (beaten on the feet) by a hireling, and forced, as a consequence, into an enormously fruitful three-year exile to "London". Six years after the events described, Voltaire retired to the Chateau de Cirey, in the Champagne district of France ("Reims"). Voltaire arguably did more than any other single person to bring about the French Revolution, which saw both the nobility and the Crown succumbing to the "Etruscan plague".

Charles Darwin

DATE 1831, CENTURY IV, QUATRAIN 31

"La Lune au plain de nuict sus [sur] le haut mont
Le nouveau sophe d'un seul cerveau la [l'a] veu:
Par ses disciples estre immortel semond,
Yeux au mydi, en seins mains, corps au feu."

The full moon will be seen at night on the high mountain
By the solitary, newly-fledged scholar
Thanks to his disciples, his teachings become immortal
His eyes turned to the southern hemisphere, hands on chest, they immolate his body.

On 27 December 1831, the recently graduated Charles Darwin made his way up the gangplank of HMS *Beagle*, and towards the Galapagos Islands, the "southern hemisphere", and a unique place in the history of science and of humanity. As a result of his five-year voyage, Darwin (1809–82) posited that species originated through evolutionary change, natural selection, and common descent, rather than through divine intervention or the catastrophe theory. His 1859 book *On The Origin Of Species* has since proved to be one of the most influential of the 19th century, and disciples of Darwinism such as John Burdon Haldane, Sewell Wright, Julian Huxley and Richard Dawkins, have fanned the flames of evolutionary theory ever since ("thanks to his disciples, his teachings become immortal"). Nostradamus correctly describes Darwin's theory of evolution in terms of a gradual revelation from darkness into light, triggered by his researches and passion for the southern hemisphere. The quatrain is also accurate in describing Darwin as a "solitary, newly-fledged scholar". In view of line four, it

might be interesting to point out that the first formal cremation in the United States took place in Washington, Pennsylvania, on 6 December 1876 – the body was that of Baron Joseph Henry Louis de Palm, and its "immolation" was accompanied by readings from Charles Darwin and from the Hindu scriptures. Darwin was one of only five 19th-century non-royals to be honoured with a state funeral. He is buried at Westminster Abbey very near to both John Herschel (1792–1871) and Isaac Newton (1643–1727). Nostradamus's final, extraordinary image of Darwin's eyes "still turned towards the southern hemisphere" even in death, suitably sums up this epoch-changing man.

Albert Einstein

DATE 1905, CENTURY III, QUATRAIN 5

"Pres loing defaut de deux grands luminaires,
Qui surviendra entre l'Avril et Mars
O quel cherté! Mais deux grans debonnaires,
Par terre et mer secourrant toutes pars."

Two great luminaries, both near and far, are blemished
This will occur some time between April and March
Oh what a terrible cost! But two great gentlemen
Will assist all parties, both by land and sea.

The "two great luminaries" are the sun (far) and the moon (near), so we can assume, when Nostradamus talks of a "blemish", that he is implying both an eclipse and an alchemical *conjunctio* that has gone slightly wrong. Given the index date of 5, it seems that the eclipse Nostradamus is referring to, and that occurred "between April and March" (one presumes of the following index-dated year), must be the total solar eclipse of 30 August 1905. Now given the date, 1905, and Nostradamus's concern with both alchemy and light, we find ourselves inexorably led towards Albert Einstein – for 1905 was known as his *annus mirabilis*, on account of the two great papers he published, on 17 March and 30 June respectively, that were to lay the groundwork for quantum physics. But Nostradamus speaks of "two great gentlemen". Well the other must surely be Albert Einhorn, the eminent German chemist who first effectively synthesized the wonder drug Novocaine (procaine hydrochloride) in 1905, and which is still in use today as a dental anaesthetic.

Scopes Monkey Trial

DATE 1925, CENTURY I, QUATRAIN 25

"Perdu, trouvé, caché de si long siecle
Sera pasteur demi dieu honore,
Ainsi que la lune achève son grand cycle
Par autres veux sera deshonoré."

Lost, found, hidden for so many centuries
The pastor will be honoured as a demigod
Just as the moon completes her great cycle
Others will wish to disgrace him.

Many commentators have leapt with glee onto the Louis Pasteur (1822–95) bandwagon when faced with this quatrain – after all, the word *"pasteur"* is clearly used in line two, and therefore the French father of microbiology must surely be the demigod referred to in the text? Well, mustn't he? Actually, no. To a person of Nostradamus's generation, the word *pasteur* would have had the clear meaning of a protestant minister, stemming, as it does, from the French word for "shepherd". With this in mind, and given the index date of 25, a far more interesting reading of the quatrain comes to light. For May 1925 saw the infamous Scopes Monkey Trial, in which hot-shot lawyers Clarence Darrow and William Henry Bryan faced up to each other in the unlikely setting of the Rhea County courthouse in Dayton, Tennessee, to dispute the legitimacy of teaching Darwin's theory of evolution to young children. At the end of the eight-day hearing the (inevitably biased) jury took a mere nine minutes to decide in favour of the religious fundamentalists.

Berlin Olympics

DATE 1936, CENTURY IV, QUATRAIN 36

"Les ieux nouveau en Gaule redresses,
Après victoire de l'Insubre champaigne:
Monts d'Esperie, les grands liés, troussés:
De peur trembler la Romaigne & l'Espaigne."

The new games are as a straightened switch
After the victory of the Insubrian campaign
The Western Mountains, the great tied and bound
Both Spain and Romania tremble in fear.

Line one sees Nostradamus having great fun punning on the word
"Gaule", which can mean either "France", or a "pole" or "switch" –
the word *"redresses"* provides us with our clue to the pun, however,
for to *redresser un baton* is common French usage for "to straighten a
stick", and leads us to the bundled sticks, known as fasces, with which
the Romans preceded any triumph or communal games, and which
were symbolically used throughout 20th-century fascism (particularly
in the case of the "Insubrians" – Milan, Pavia, etc. – whose Fascists
used the fasces as their main symbol). The notion of "new games",
too, is a powerful one, as Paris hosted the Olympic Games of 1900 and
1924, and in 1936 (*see* index date), those games were handed over to
Berlin, which, subsequent to the initial allocation of the games (which
occurred, pre-Hitler, in 1931), now housed the German Fascist Party.
The year 1936 saw fascism on the rise in both Romania and in Spain,
where the Civil War was to break out on 17 July, just two weeks before
the formal opening ceremony for the summer Olympics. Hitler and

his National Socialist Party later hijacked the Games, with the help of propagandist filmmaker Leni Riefenstahl, in order to showcase their theories of Aryan racial supremacy – something which spectacularly backfired on them (and the segregationist United States) when the African American sprinter Jesse Owens won four gold medals. A remarkable quatrain, therefore, depicting the 1936 Berlin summer Olympics as linked to the rise of fascism and to the temporary stultification of the Western Powers – Nostradamus's image of those same powers "tied and bound", with the Olympics functioning as a "switch" to beat them with, is a memorable one.

HEROINES, HOYDENS and HARLOTS

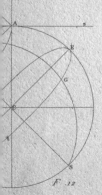

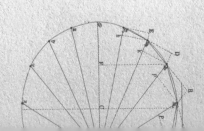

Elizabeth I

DATE 1558, CENTURY X, QUATRAIN 84

"La naturelle à si hault hault non bas
Le tard retour fera marris contens,
Le Recloing ne sera sans debatz
En empliant et pendant tout son temps."

The natural daughter, not low at all, is set so very high
This late comeback will please the apologists
The secret will be much debated
Both in the filling, and during all of her tenure.

England's King Henry VIII married Spain's Catherine of Aragon on 11 June 1509. Catherine bore Henry two short-lived sons and a longer-lived daughter, Mary, who became his heir – and as far as the Catholic Church was concerned, that was that (despite Catherine's formerly having been married to Henry's brother, Arthur, who had died a bare six months after the wedding). But Henry wanted a male heir, and commenced formal proceedings to have the marriage annulled on account of the previous consummation with his brother (which Catherine vehemently denied). When his mistress, Anne Boleyn, unexpectedly fell pregnant, Henry speeded up proceedings by dismantling the Roman Catholic Church in England, establishing a Protestant (and considerably more amenable) alternative. Thus, when Elizabeth (later to be Queen Elizabeth I) was born, the entire Catholic world believed her to be Henry's bastard ("natural") daughter, with no technical rights to the throne of England. The recriminations continued throughout Elizabeth's reign ("during all of her tenure").

Catherine de Medici

"La Dame seule au regne demeurée
L'unic esteint premier au lict d'honneur:
Sept ans sera de douleur explorée,
Puis longue vie au regne par grand heur."

The widowed Lady will remain in the kingdom
Her only husband will die first on the field of honour
Seven years will be put aside for mourning
The realm will endure for a long time in greatness.

On 25 March 1552 Henri II declared his wife, Catherine de Medici, regent, either in his absence or in the event of his premature death. Seven years later Henri died in a freak accident whilst jousting, and this foresight became reality. It was at that time customary for mourning queens to remain in their dead husband's bedchamber for 40 days and nights with no light other than that of wax tapers. Catherine – although nominally devoted to her husband despite his many years of open dalliance with the 17-year-older-than-himself Diane de Poitiers (who had also been his father's mistress) – contrived to avoid this fate by removing the court from Paris to St Germain under the pretext of protecting her son, Charles IX, from Protestant heretics. The date 1563 refers to the end of Charles's minority, when Catherine should have handed the power of the State over to her son – in practice, of course, she dominated him during his entire reign. The Royal French Realm, despite Nostradamus's line four, was to endure for only a further 226 years.

The Casket Letters

DATE 1569, CENTURY VIII, QUATRAIN 23

"Lettres trouvees de la roine les coffres,
Point de subscrit sans aucun nom d'hauteur
Par la police seront caché les offres,
Qu'on ne scaura qui sera l'amateur."

Letters attributed to the queen are found in a casket
They bear neither signature nor author's name
The government conceals the offers within them
So that no one will know who is responsible.

It is at least conceivable that Nostradamus actually met the 14-year-old Mary Queen of Scots when he found himself summoned by Catherine de Medici to appear at the French court in 1556. Catherine was to become Mary's mother-in-law in 1558, through the marriage to Mary of her son, the dauphin (later François II). The marriage was short-lived, thanks to François's death only 17 months after that of his father, Henri II. François died of a purported ear infection, a misadventure that led directly to Mary's return to Scotland and to the tragic chain of events that followed, and which were to include the episode of the so-called "casket letters". The grammatically poor letters (Mary was a fluent French speaker) appeared as if from nowhere, and seemed designed to implicate Mary in the murder of her second husband, Lord Darnley. Somewhat surprisingly, in the circumstances, Mary found herself exonerated at the formal enquiry. Despite this, Mary's cousin, Elizabeth I, retained Mary in "protective custody" for the next 18 years, until her execution for treason in 1587.

La Reine Margot

"Le pere & filz seront meurdris ensemble
Le prefecteur dedans son pavillon
La mere à Tours du filz ventre aura enfle.
Caiche verdure de feuilles papillon."

Father and son will be murdered together
The one set over another is in his pavilion
The son causes the mother's belly to swell at Tours
A chest full of herbs and twisted paper.

Line three is a difficult one, and could be read two ways – either that the mother is carrying a son in the normal manner, or that the son has impregnated his own mother. Line four, too, suggests a herbalist's trunk with paper put aside for wrapping prescriptions. One might be tempted to ascribe the last two lines to an unwanted pregnancy, therefore, and an attempt at an abortion with herbs. The *"prefecteur"* also gives us pause for thought, as there is no such French word, and the Latin, *praefectus*, implies one person set over another (i.e. it suggests the act of coition). Marguerite de Valois (a.k.a. La Reine Margot) was 22 years old in 1575, and already earning a well-deserved reputation as a promiscuous, and possibly incestuous adulteress (she had married Henri IV three years before, and he tolerated her affairs, whilst conducting numerous of his own). Might the abortion relate to her? Interested parties should read Marguerite de Navarre's *The Heptameron* (1558) for further salacious revelations about the private lives of kings and courtiers.

Barbara Blomberg

DATE 1578, CENTURY IX, QUATRAIN 78

"La dame Grecque de beauté laydique,
Heureuse faicte de procs innumerable,
Hors translatee au regne Hispanique,
Captive prinse mourir mort miserable."

The Greek lady with the beauty of Lais
Is made very happy by her innumerable lovers
She is snatched away to the Kingdom of Spain
The captive prince dies a miserable death.

"Lais" (*Laidis* in Latin) was a famous courtesan ("*proc*", in line two, is an abbreviation of *procureuse*, a bawd). Lais was "snatched away" from her native home to Greece, following Nicias the Athenian's invasion of Sicily. She later took "innumerable lovers", and was assassinated in the Temple of Venus, in Thessaly, circa 340 BC, by a delegation of angry, jilted wives. This modern version of Lais is probably Barbara Blomberg, the courtesan mother of Catholic hero Don John of Austria (his natural father was Holy Roman Emperor Charles V). Despite receiving a large state pension on Don John's behalf, she publicly disowned him as her son. Barbara Blomberg, like Lais, was indeed "snatched away to the Kingdom of Spain", for she had been destined for Italy and respectability by Don John, but for some reason her ship contrived to turn around at the very last moment, whisking her to the Spanish estate of her new lover, Don John's private secretary, Juan de Escobedo (who was himself assassinated by *bravos* on Easter Monday that same year).

Mary Queen of Scots

DATE 1587, CENTURY X, QUATRAIN 19

"Jour que sera par roine saluee,
Le jour apres le salut, la priere,
Le compte fait raison et valbuee,
Par avant humbles oncques ne feut si fiere."

One day she will be acknowledged as a queen
The very next day she will pray
The reckoning is a right and a good one
Above all humble, never was there one so proud.

A direct follow-on to 8/23 – 1569: The Casket Letters, the Catholic Nostradamus would most probably have viewed the execution of Mary, Queen of Scots, by the Protestant Elizabeth I as martyrdom at best, and *lèse majesté* at worst. Mary was only told of her execution at dinner the night before it was due to take place. She was, in addition, denied the comfort of her own chaplain and the last sacrament, her warders being most insistent (for obvious reasons) that she avail herself of a Protestant minister instead. The execution was appallingly botched, in that an anointed queen required three blows from the headsman before the decapitation was complete. Just before the beheading, Mary had thrown off her black cloak to reveal a deep-red dress, the traditional liturgical colour symbolizing martyrdom in the Catholic Church. Mary's remains were later embalmed and sealed in an above-ground lead casket to prevent the taking of relics for, although she was never formally canonized by the Roman Catholic Church, many Catholics considered Mary a martyr in the Church's cause.

Pocahontas

DATE 1607, CENTURY I, QUATRAIN 7

"Tard arrivé l'execution faicte,
Le vent contraire, lettres au chemin prinses
Les conjures xiiij. d'une secte,
Par le Rosseau senez les entreprinses."

Late arrived, but the thing is done
The wind was against them, letters were taken en route
The oath-takers xiiij, all of one sect
The wise red-haired man will take them under his wing.

An extraordinary quatrain, date perfect, and clearly alluding to the landing, on 26 April 1607, of the English colonists at Jamestown, Virginia, close to where they went on to found the first permanent English colony in North America under a month later, on 14 May (*see* Nostradamus's "xiiij" [i.e. 14 in Roman numerals where i and j are interchangeable] in line three). Nostradamus beautifully describes their "late arrival" – the journey of the three ships, the *Susan Constant*, *The Discovery*, and *The Godspeed*, had taken a crippling five months, which was far longer than the usual crossing. The most fascinating part of the prophecy comes next, however, with the appearance of the "wise red-haired man". Captain John Smith, one of the leaders of the colonists, was captured whilst searching for food along the banks of the Chickahominy River. He was taken to see Wahunsonacock, Chief of the Powhatans, at his main camp at Werewocomoco. There follows the famous story of John Smith's brush with death, and the saving of his life thanks to the physical intercession of Pocahontas (then aged

11 or 12), the daughter of the chief, who threw herself across his body, and "at the minute of my execution, she hazarded the beating out of her own brains to save mine". John Smith later described the costume of an Indian chief in the following manner: "...with a crown of deer's hair, coloured red...his body was painted all with crimson, with a chain of beads about his neck." The "red-haired" chief did indeed take Captain John Smith "under his wing", ordering him, at the behest of his daughter, to be safely accompanied back to the colony at Jamestown. Never romantically involved with Smith, Pocahontas later went on to marry Englishman John Rolfe, by whom she had a son.

Empress Meishō

DATE 1629, CENTURY VI, QUATRAIN 29

"La veuve saincte entendant les nouvelles,
De ses rameaux mis en perplex & trouble:
Qui sera duict appaiser les querelles,
Par son pourchas des razes fera comble."

The saintly widow hearing the news
Of her branches in perplexity and trouble
He who will be best suited to pacify the quarrellers
Will over-egg the pudding in his pursuit of the shaved ones.

The "saintly widow" is Empress Meishō (1624–96), who succeeded her father, Go-Mizunoo (1596–1680), as empress of Japan in 1629, after the notorious "purple clothes incident", in which the emperor had been formally accused by the shogun (who held the real power) of bestowing honorific purple robes on ten banned priests (the "shaved ones"). Go-Mizunoo abruptly abdicated, ensuring that the Empress Meishō (whose personal name was Okiko) became only the 7th woman to sit on the Chrysanthemum Throne, and the 109th monarch of Japan. She reigned until 1643 but remained childless, and was succeeded by her younger half-brother, Emperor Go-Kōmyō, when she finally abdicated. It is believed that during her reign, her father ruled in all but name, thanks to the intrinsically male-orientated hierarchic organization of the Japanese imperial court (a situation which still adheres to this day). The empress was renowned for her exquisite taste in garden ornamentation and design, and she used much of her great personal wealth in the cause of aesthetics.

Queen Christina

DATE 1644, CENTURY II, QUATRAIN 44

"L'aigle pousée en tour des pavillions
Par autres oyseaux d'entour sera chassée,
Quand bruit des cymbres, tubes & sonaillons,
Rendront le sens de la dame insensée."

The she-eagle is pushed back around the pavilions
She is mobbed by birds of another locality
Where the noise of cymbals, trumpets and fanfares
Brings the foolish lady back to her senses.

The "she-eagle" is Queen Christina of Sweden, who was brought up like a boy by her father, King Gustav II Adolf, even to the extent of wearing male apparel and riding astride. This fad of her father's became such common knowledge that she was called the Girl-King by her future subjects. In 1644 (*see* index date) Christina reached her majority, having been queen regnant since her father's death in 1632. During the next ten years, Christina did appear to "lose her senses", given that she created 17 counts, 46 barons and 428 lesser nobles, pretty much bankrupting the exchequer in so doing. She eventually converted to Catholicism, and abdicated in favour of Charles X, as a Catholic queen would have been an impossibility in Lutheran Sweden. She left, dressed as a man, on a boat bound for Rome ("she is mobbed by birds of another locality"), where she was received by Pope Alexander VII with extraordinary fanfare and pomp ("where the noise of cymbals, trumpets and fanfares brings the foolish lady back to her senses").

Queen Anne

DATE 1702, CENTURY IV, QUATRAIN 96

"La soeur aisnee de l'isle Britannique,
Quinze ans devant le frère aura naissance:
Par son promis moyennant verrifique,
Succedera au regne de Balance."

The older sister of the British Isles
Fifteen years before her brother will be born
By means of his true promise
She will succeed to the Libran crown.

Elizabeth I was only four years "older" than her "brother", Edward VI, but he certainly didn't "promise" her the throne. His "sister" Mary is a better bet, being born 21 years before him, but Edward still did everything in his power to make sure that she was disinherited. We have the perfect match, however, in King William III and his sister-in-law, Queen Anne (the sister of his wife and co-ruler, Mary), particularly given the ambiguity of the text, which can be read in either of two fashions. William was born on 14 November 1650, and Anne on 6 February 1665 ("fifteen years before, her brother will be born" – the translation is exact, and only the comma has been added for emphasis). Anne duly ascended to the throne in 1702, a mere six years after Nostradamus's index date of 96. In addition, the sign of "Libra" occurs between 22 September and 22 October, when both day and night are equal. Anne succeeded to a crown in which both male (day) and female (night) were equally balanced.

Queen Victoria

"Ce grand monarque qu'au mort succedera,
Donnera vie illicite et lubrique,
Par nonchalance à tous concedera,
Qu'à la parfin fauldra la loy Salique."

The great monarch who inherits after death
Will give life to the illicit and the lubricious
By nonchalance he concedes to all
That at the end-passing, Salic law will be needed.

"Salic law" (the *Lex Salica*) was codified during the reign of King Clovis I, around 507–11. It was multicultural, defining which law a person adhered to by virtue of their differing race or ethnicity. The most controversial part of the law concerned the prohibition on women from inheriting any Salic land whatsoever, unless their father had no surviving sons. The implication in this quatrain, therefore, is that a woman comes to the throne who should not – and would not – were Salic law in force. Could this be about Queen Victoria, then, who came to the throne in 1837 (one year off the index date), and whose son, Edward VII, was a renowned roisterer and libertine ("will give life to the illicit and the lubricious")? The accession of Queen Victoria to the throne of England in 1837 was fortunately not scuppered by Salic law. She was, however, prevented from taking the throne of Hanover by Salic law, being forced to make way for the Duke of Cumberland, the oldest surviving grandson of King George II.

Isabel Perón

DATE 1974, CENTURY VI, QUATRAIN 74

"La deschassee au regne tournera,
Ses ennemis trouvés des conjurés:
Plus que jamais son temps triomphera,
Trois et septante à mort trop asseurés."

The exiled woman returns to reign
Her enemies are found amongst the conspirators
Her era will be more triumphal than ever
Three and seventy are known to have died.

This is the return from exile of Isabel (Isabelita) Perón to Argentina on 29 June 1974, following the illness of the president, her husband (the immensely popular Juan Perón, progenitor of the Argentinean Peronist movement's so-called "third way", designed to fill the gap between capitalism and socialism). With her husband effectively *hors de combat*, Isabelita was elected President of Argentina in her own right on 1 July 1974, nearly a year to the day following the Ezeiza Massacre which succeeded in toppling Perón's predecessor and friend, Héctor Cámpora (*El Tio*), from power. Isabel, a former nightclub dancer, was incapable of managing a state in such a complicated and dangerous condition as Argentina at that time, and despite first receiving assurances of support from the army, she was later kidnapped, placed under house arrest for five years, and then deported to Spain by the proto-fascist clique responsible for ousting her. The arbitrary manner of Isabelita's downfall arguably paved the way for the eventual rejection of totalitarianism by the Argentine people.

Death of Princess Di

DATE 1997, CENTURY IV, QUATRAIN 97

"L'an que Mercure, Mars, Venus retrograde
Du grand Monarque la ligne ne faillit:
Esleu du peuple l'usitant pres de Gagdole,
Qu'en paix et regne viendra fort envieillir."

In the same year that Mercury, Mars and Venus retrograde
The grand-monarch's line will not fail
Chosen by the people, the very well-known person was close to Gagdole
Both peace and reign will age him.

"Mercury", "Mars", and "Venus" are three of the five planets (alongside Jupiter and Saturn) that are, technically at least, visible to the naked eye. In astrology, "Mars retrograde" suggests a frigid person, possibly prone to extremes of behaviour; "Venus retrograde" intensifies this reading, taking the sex aversion even further until it becomes deleterious to married life; and "Mercury retrograde" furthers the disruption, giving rise to unforced errors, travel chaos, and relational misunderstandings. Given the index date of 97, we find that Mercury, Mars, and Venus all retrograded in 1997, with Mercury, in particular, retrograding in the days surrounding the death, following a car accident, of Britain's Diana, Princess of Wales ("*l'usitant*", in line three, may represent an elision of *usitée*, meaning "well known", and *tant*, meaning "very"). The "grand-monarch's line" will most likely be that of Queen Victoria, grandam to countless descendants. We may therefore assume that "*Gagdole*" relates to Prince Charles, given that *gage* in Old French, means "a pledge", and *dol* means "deceit".

Diana & Dodi

DATE 2012, CENTURY IX, QUATRAIN 12

"Le tant d'argent de Diane & Mercure
Les simulacres au lac seront trouvez,
Le figulier cherchant argille neufve
Luy & les siens d'or seront abbrevez."

Despite all the money of Diana and Mercury
Their empty shadows will be found at the lake
For the potter in search of new clay
He and his people will be drenched with gold.

"Diana", Princess of Wales, and her lover, Dodi Fayed, were killed in a car crash in Paris, early on the morning of 31 August 1997. Diana's brother, Lord Spencer, oversaw the building of a water park at their natal Althorp Estate in honour of her life, and Diana's "empty shadow" is indeed buried on an island, on the lake, with Dodi's shadow forever bound up with hers. Dodi Fayed is associated with "Mercury", in line one, for Mercury was the Roman god of trade, and both Dodi and his father, Mohammed al Fayed, owner of Harrods, London's world-famous department store, owed their fortunes to commerce. Ancient American Indian lore has it that we are all made of "clay" (*see* line three), and that Manitou simply baked the white man for too short a period, and the black man for too long a period – the red man he baked just right. This concept (with the usual variations, depending on self-interest) runs through many religions, and Romans ix. 21, is particularly succinct on the matter: "Hath not the potter power over the clay, of the same lump to make one vessel unto honour, and another

unto dishonour?" The concept of "gold" inevitably leads us back to Midas, King of Phrygia, and his request to the gods that everything he touch be turned to gold. Lady Diana Spencer made a similar request by marrying Prince Charles, heir to the British throne, and so, in his way, did Dodi Fayed, when he took up with the golden-haired Diana. Nostradamus appears to be saying that all the money and fame in the world are no longer of use to them – all that remains are their empty shadows in the memorial water park at Althorp.

THE FUTURE FORETOLD

The Third Antichrist
A Pan-African Leader
Nostradamus's Goodbye

The Third Antichrist

DATE 2035, CENTURY III, QUATRAIN 35

"Du plus profond de l'Occident d'Europe,
De pauvres gens un ieune enfant naistra,
Qui par sa langue seduira grande troupe:
Son bruit au regne d'Orient plus croistra."

From deep in the Western part of Europe
A child will be born, to poor parents
He will seduce the multitude with his tongue
The noise of his reputation will grow in the Eastern kingdom.

This new leader of the Eastern/Muslim world will be around 35 years old by the time of the global war referred to in Nostradamus's quatrain 5/70 – 2070 ("From the regions governed by Libra / A great war will come, enough to disturb the mountains / Both sexes will be captured, and all Byzantium / So that cries will be heard at dawn, from country to country"). Though only from a humble background in the western Islamic diaspora, the Third Antichrist – the first two Antichrists being Napoleon Bonaparte and Adolf Hitler – will pull

together the equivalent of the old Ottoman Empire by the seductive power of his language, and threaten the dominant positions of the US and China. This will result in a catastrophic nuclear war, "powerful enough to disturb mountains". The worrying aspect of this quatrain lies in the word "*seduira*", "to seduce" or deceive by charm, in line three, with its implication that this leader will be a manipulator and a fixer, and also in the word "*bruit*", in line four, implying that his reputation will be spun as a form of narrative, rather than fairly earned. It's a worrying quatrain in every respect, and echoes the presage about Adolf Hitler, as the Second Antichrist, in the now famous "wild beasts" quatrain (*see* 2/24 – 1945). This is the closest that Nostradamus ever came to a categorical warning to the world about a future potential holocaust, and the subtle language he uses here echoes this, with its hints of hidden depths and secret manipulations. Nostradamus is telling us that the Third Antichrist is now born. The die has been cast. The future of the world, unless a miracle occurs, will be very bleak, with global warfare and ecological damage occurring on an unprecedented scale.

A Pan-African Leader

DATE 2041, CENTURY V, QUATRAIN 41

"Nay soubs les umbres & journee nocturne
Sera en regne & bonté souveraine:
Fera renaistre son sang de l'antique urne,
Renouvellant siecle d'or pour l'aerain."

Born inside the shadows, on the very day of an eclipse
He will be sovereign in rule and goodness
He will renew his blood at the ancient urn
Restoring the golden age with bronze.

The total eclipse Nostradamus mentions in line one covers Angola, the Congo, Uganda, Kenya, and Somalia, and not western Europe, so it is of a great Pan-African leader that we are talking here, who will unite traditionally disparate tribes and countries, affording Africa, for only the second time in its post-colonial history, a significant influence for good on the world stage. This reading is further strengthened by Nostradamus's use of the expression "ancient urn" in line three, for we now know that Africa, and in particular the geographical areas comprised within Kenya and Tanzania, was, in all probability, the cradle of human life. "Bronze", too, has its role to play in this reading, as it was one of the earliest known alloys, and is cast on a bed of clay. The strong implication in line four, then, is that we need to revert back to the simplicities and certainties of the past in order to be able to renew the future, and that the great Pan-African leader Nostradamus speaks of here will achieve this miracle.

Nostradamus's Goodbye

DATE 7048, CENTURY I, QUATRAIN 48

"Vingt ans du regne de la lune passés,
Sept mil ans autre tiendra sa monarchie:
Quand le soleil prendra ses iours lassés,
Lors accomplir a mine ma prophetie.."

Twenty years after the moon's reign is over
Another monarch will take over for seven thousand years
When the sun finally takes its leave
My deep prophesying will be accomplished.

The "moon" (*móna*) in Anglo-Saxon means a "measurer" of time. In Sanskrit, Gothic, Old French, and Greek, the moon was viewed in a similar way, and in the true tradition of right-brain (insight, imagination, musicality, art awareness, 3-D forms, left-hand control) and left-brain (reasoning, science, language, number skills, right-hand control) functionality, it was considered a masculine and left-brained, rather than a feminine and right-brained force, by, amongst others, the Arabians, the Slavs, the Hindus, the Mexicans and the Lithuanians. The "sun", on the other hand, and particularly in Celtic and low-Breton mythology, took on a feminine aspect, and lived in perpetual fear of being eaten by the wolf, Fenris (hence eclipses). The Celts believed that the sun would one day have a daughter, who would reign in her stead, rekindling the life force of a weary world. Nostradamus is now telling us that the human period in world affairs is coming to an end. It has lasted for a very short time, and will leave no imprint of its passing. Nature will fill the vacuum.

Selective
Bibliography

Benazra, Robert, *Répertoire chronologique Nostradamique*, (Maisnie Tredaniel, France 1990)

Benedict, Gerald, *The Watkins Dictionary of Religions and Secular Faiths* (Watkins 2008)

Boyer, Paul S. (Ed.) *The Oxford Companion to United States History* (Oxford University Press 2001)

Brind'Amour, Pierre, *Nostradamus Astrophile* (Kincksieck/University of Ottawa, 1993)
Nostradamus: Les Premières Centuries ou Prophéties (Droz, 1996)

Chomarat, Michel, and Laroche, Jean-Paul: *Bibliographie Nostradamus* (Baden-Baden and Bouxwiller 1989)

Clébert, Jean-Paul, *Prophéties de Nostradamus* (Relié-Dervy, 2003)

Cruden, Alexander, *A Complete Concordance to the Old and New Testament or a Dictionary and Alphabetical Index to the Bible* (Frederick Warne and Co., Ltd., of London and New York. 1737–69)

Doyle, William (ed.), *The Oxford History of the French Revolution* (Oxford University Press USA 2002)

Dufresne, Michel, *Dictionnaire Nostradamus* (Chicoutimi, Québec, 1989)

Dupèbe, Jean, *Nostradamus: Lettres inédites* (Librairie Droz, Geneva 1983)

Emmerson, Richard Kenneth, *Antichrist in the Middle Ages: A Study of Medieval Apocalypticism, Art, and Literature* (University of Washington Press 1981)

Fuller, Robert, *Naming The Antichrist: The History of an American Obsession* (Oxford University Press USA, 1996)

Gilbert, Martin, *A History of the Twentieth Century* (Harper Perennial 2002)
The Second World War: A Complete History (Holt Paperbacks 2004)

Gruber, Elmar, *Nostradamus: Sein Leben, Sein Werk und die wahre Bedeutung seiner Prophezeiungen* (Scherz, 2003)

Jung, C. G., *Answer to Job* (Routledge & Kegan Paul, London, 1954)
Aion (Routledge & Kegan Paul, London, 1959)

Kennedy, David M. (Ed.), *The Oxford History of the United States* – multiple volumes (Oxford University Press USA)

Kinross, Lord, *The Ottoman Centuries: The Rise and Fall of the Turkish Empire* (Harper Perennial 1979)

Lake, Peter (with Michael Questier), *The Antichrist's Lewd Hat* (Yale University Press 2002)

Lempriere, J., *Lempriere's Classical Dictionary* (Bracken Books 1984)

Leroy, Dr Edgar, *Nostradamus, Ses Origines, Sa Vie, Son Oeuvre*, (1972 – reprinted Saint-Rémy de Provence, Laffitte 1993)

Marsden, Hilary (Ed.) *Chambers Dictionary of World History* (Chambers Harrap Edinburgh 2005)

McGinn, Bernard, *Visions of the End* (Columbia University Press, 1998)
Antichrist (Columbia University Press, 2000)

Reading, Mario, *Nostradamus: The Complete Prophecies for the Future* (Watkins 2006)
Nostradamus: The Good News (Watkins 2007)
The Complete Prophecies of Nostradamus (Watkins 2009)

Roberts, J. M., *The New History of the World* (Oxford University Press UK & USA 2003)

Russell, Jeffrey Burton, *The Prince of Darkness: Radical Evil and the Power of Good in History* (Cornell University Press, 1992)
Lucifer: The Devil in the Middle Ages (Cornell University Press 1984)
Witchcraft in the Middle Ages (Cornell University Press 1972)

Shirer, William L., *The Rise and Fall of the Third Reich* (Simon & Schuster 1990)

Williams, Hywel, *Cassell's Chronology of World History* (Weidenfeld & Nicolson 2005)

Wilson, Ian, *Nostradamus: The Evidence* (Orion, London 2002)
The Man Behind The Prophecies (St Martin's Griffin 2007)

Index

Acknowledgments

Any illustrated book derives its life-source not only from the author's original text, but also from a multitude of often unrecognized aiders and abetters who, by a process of quasi-alchemical osmosis, contribute to the success of the finished article. I would like to thank my editorial director, Bob Saxton, Paul Reid at Cobalt ID who commissioned the artwork, the artist Nicky Ackland-Snow, the picture researcher Julia Ruxton, designer Luana Gobbo, art director Roger Walton, Christopher Westhorp for his historical expertise on the artwork, and my perennial copy editor Shelagh Boyd. This book is a credit to you all.

For my late mother-in-law
Irma (Mima) Fernandez de Fautsch

Picture credits
The publisher would like to thank the following people, museums and photographic libraries for permission to reproduce their material. Every care has been taken to trace copyright holders. However, if we have omitted anyone we apologize and will, if informed, make corrections to any future edition.

Pictures are listed by letter from left to right in rows starting from the top of each page

45 Princes, Presidents & Plunderers: a Philip II Spain and Portugal (Getty Images/Imagno); **b** William III of England (Getty Images/Popperfoto); **c** James I of England (akg-images/© Sotheby's); **d** Frederick the Great (Getty Images/SuperStock); **e** George Washington (iStock/N. Staykov); **f** Napoleon Bonaparte (iStock/Getty Images/Hulton Archive); **g** George IV of England (akg-images); **h** Vladimir Ilich Lenin (Corbis/Bettmann); **i** General Francisco Franco (Getty Images/Keystone); **j** HRH Edward, Prince of Wales (Getty Images/Popperfoto); **k** Adolf Hitler (Getty Images/Heinrich Hoffmann); **l** Nicolas Sarkozy (Corbis/Kipa/ © Christophe Russeil/Kipa); **67 Murders, Massacres & Machinations: a** Suleiman II, Sultan of Turkey (Getty Images/Bridgeman Art Library/Schloss Ambras, Austria); **b** Henri II, of France (Getty Images/Hulton Archive/Imagno/Musee Crozatier, Le Puy); **c** Man dying of the plague, 14th-15th century (Photolibrary.com/Imagestate/The British Library); **d** The Defenestration of Prague (Theatrum Europaeum); **e** Charles I of England (Philip Mould Ltd/Historical Portraits Image Library); **f** Charles XII of Sweden (Private Collection); **g** The assassination of President Lincoln (Library of Congress); **h** Night of the Long Knives, Munich, 9. Nov. 1923, Group photo: Hermann Kriebel, Erich Ludendorff, Adolf Hitler, Wilhelm Brückner, Ernst Röhm (Deutsches Bundesarchiv/Foto Hoffmann); **i** Charles de Gaulle (Getty Images/Agence France Presse); **j** A Montagnard tribesman, Tieu Atar, South Vietnam, 1969 (Corbis/Bettmann); **k** President and Mrs. John F. Kennedy minutes before he was assassinated, November 22, 1963 (Corbis/Bettmann); **83 Revolution, Riots & Rapine: a** Conspiracy of Amboise 1560 (akg-images); **b** Charles IX France (Getty Images/Roger Viollet Collection/Versailles Museum); **c** Francis I of France (Corbis/© Fine Art Photographic Library); **d** Spanish Dutch War 1568-1648 - Attack on Antwerp by Duke François d'Anjou (akg-images/British Library); **e** Guy Fawkes and associates, 1606 (Private Collection); **f** Storming of the Bastille, 1789 (Musée National du Château de Versailles); **g** Capture of Louis XVI on their flight to England in 1791 (akg-images); **h** E.Dollfuss at Trabrennplatz Racecourse, Vienna 1933 (akg-images/Ullstein Bild); **i** Protesting French students fighting with police in the rue Saint-Jacques in Paris, May 6, 1968 (Getty Images/AFP); **103 Enslavement, Expansion & Empire: a** Lala Mustafa Pasha in his Encampment after his Victory at Kars, Georgia in 1578 (Bridgeman Art Library/British Library Board. All Rights Reserved); **b** Queen Elizabeth I of England (Getty Images/Bridgeman Art Library/Private Collection); **c** Battle of Bunker Hill, June 17, 1775 (Getty Images/Hulton Archive); **d** Napoleon on his Imperial Throne (Musée de l'Armée, Paris); **e** Neptune Engaged, Battle of Trafalgar, 1805 (Corbis/The Gallery Collection);

f Group of Negroes, imported to be sold for slaves, 1806 (Getty Images/Bridgeman Art Library/Private Collection); **g** Simón Bolívar (Corbis/Christie's Images); **h** Gen. CG Gordon (Private Collection); **i** Mohandas K. Gandhi (Private Collection); **j** Aachen Cathedral (Corbis); **k** Guantanamo Naval Base, United States March 2002 (Getty Images/AFP/Peter Muhly); **l** Heavy Bombing in Baghdad, March 21, 2003 (Corbis/Olivier Coret); **131 Disaster, Disease & Desolation: a** Funeral of Titian, who died from plague in Venice 1576 (akg-images/Erich Lessing/Musée du Louvre, Paris); **b** Russian palace guards, or Streltsi, at the time of Peter the Great. (Photolibrary.com/North Wind Pictures); **c** Great Fire of London, September 1666 (Getty Images/Time Life Pictures/Mansell); **d** World Trade Center, New York City after the twin towers were struck by two planes during a terrorist attack September 11, 2001 (Getty Images/David Surowiecki); **e** Fire fighter standing amidst rubble and smoke after the terrorist attack on the World Trade Center, September 11, 2001 (Getty Images/Time Life Pictures/Mai/Mai); **f** New York Stock Exchange November 20, 2008 (Getty Images/Mario Tama); **g** Cracked dry mud (Getty Images/Nacivet); **h** Floods, Long Beach, California, January 2010 (Getty Images/Kevork Djansezian); **143 Heroes, Holy Men & High Hitters: a** St. John of the Cross (Getty Images/Hulton Archive); **b** Close-Up Visible Light Image of Kepler's Supernova Remnant (NASA/STScI/Hubble); **c** James VI of Scotland and I of England (Getty Images/Bridgeman Art Library/Private Collection); **d** Nostradamus (Getty Images/Time Life Pictures/Mansell); **e** Duc de Saint-Simon (Bridgeman Art Library/Lauros/Giraudon); **f** Antonio Stradivari (Getty ImagesRischgitz); **g** First page of the first part of the Christmas Oratorio, autograph score by Johann Sebastian Bach, BWV 248. 1734 (Staatsbibliothek zu Berlin, Musikabteilung); **h** François-Marie Arouet (Voltaire) (Liberal Freemason/Musée national du Château et des Trianons, Versailles); **i** Charles Darwin (J. Cameron); **j** Albert Einstein during a lecture in Vienna in 1921. (Ferdinand Schmutzer); **k** Clarence Darrow and William Jennings Bryan during the Scopes evolution trial in 1925 (Corbis/Bettmann); **l** Jesse Owens in action during 4X100 race, 15 Aug 1936, Berlin Olympics (Getty Images/Time Life Pictures); **161 Heroines, Hoydens and Harlots: a** Elizabeth I of England - The Armada Portrait (Philip Mould Ltd/Historical Portraits Image Library); **b** Catherine de' Medici, wife of Henry II of France (Private Collection); **c** Marguerite of Valois, Queen of Navarre (Berger Collection, Denver, Colorado); **d** Barbara Blomberg, mother of Don Juan of Austria, with Kaiser Karl V (Private Collection); **e** Mary Queen of Scots (Philip Mould Ltd/Historical Portraits Image Library); **f** Pocahontas (cliff1066™/National Portrait Gallery, Smithsonian Institution, Washington D.C); **g** Queen Christina of Sweden (Museo del Prado, Madrid); **h** Queen Anne of England (Philip Mould Ltd/Historical Portraits Image Library); **i** Queen Victoria of England (Philip Mould Ltd/Historical Portraits Image Library); **j** Isabel Perón (Corbis/Sygma/Diego Goldberg); **k** Diana, Princess of Wales (Getty Images/AFP/Jamal A. Wilson); **l** Fountain in memory of Diana and Dodi (Corbis/Sygma/Sion Touhig); **178 The Future Foretold: a** Nostradamus (Corbis/Bettmann).

Front cover and slipcase background: iStock

IV IX IV VII